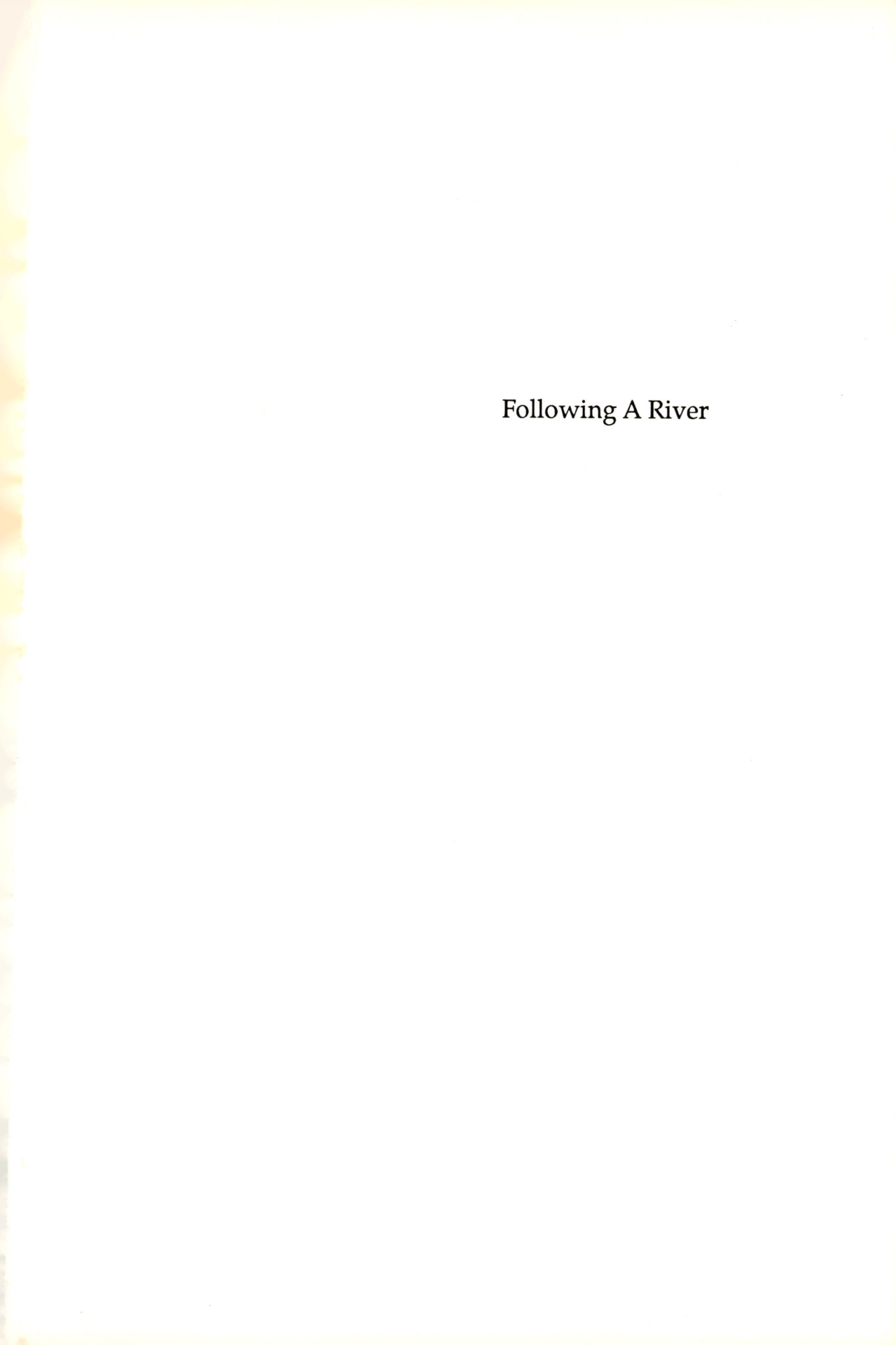

Following A River

Following A River

Portland's Congregation Neveh Shalom
1869-1989

by
Gary Miranda

based on historical research by
David Bernstein

Photograph Editor, Al Horwitz

Copyright © 1989 by Congregation Neveh Shalom

Book and colophon designed by Gary Miranda

Library of Congress Catalog Card Number: 89-081652

ISBN 0-9624962-0-0

1 2 3 4 5 6 7 8 9 10

*To the children of Neveh Shalom,
for whom the river flows*

*Freedom is not following a river.
Freedom is following a river,
though, if you want to.*

—William Stafford

Contents

Preface 1

1869-1891 / How We Got Here 7

1892-1922 / Respecting the Past 35

1923-1939 / The Disallowed Luxury 69

1940-1960 / Journeys of Chance 93

1961-1989 / The Necessary and the Possible 119

Appendices 149

Preface

That a former Jesuit seminarian should be asked to write the 120th-anniversary history of a Jewish congregation is itself enough to give us pause, if pause is what we want at the beginning of such a book. Why a Catholic rather than a Jew? Why, for that matter, 120 years rather than 100?

I can't answer the first question; you must ask the Neveh Shalom 120th Anniversary Committee, which made that decision. My interest in raising the question at all is to point out what such a choice tells us about the congregation whose history we are pausing before. I find it a remarkable choice for a Jewish congregation—not to mention for a committee, that entity justly famous for unimaginative decisions—to come up with. From what I have learned in writing the history of Neveh Shalom, I can safely guess that such a choice would have been highly unlikely 50 years ago, when the term "conservative" described the collective temperament as well as the religious bent of the congregation. What the choice confirms is that Congregation Neveh Shalom has matured to a level of self-confidence that allows it to risk the implausible, even in a matter that touches upon its self-image as closely as does this history. Whom you select to write your biography is at least as revealing as anything that a biography might disclose, and what Neveh Shalom's choice reveals is entirely to its credit.

Nor need I spend much time answering the second question—why a 120-year history?—since the majority of Jewish readers will know that 120 is the age that the Torah ascribes to Moses at the time of his death, a point reflected in the traditional Jewish good wish, "May you live to 120." The point here is to highlight the extent of my own ignorance about things Jewish when I agreed to undertake this project. I had to *ask*, "Why 120?" I also had to ask about the difference between Orthodox and Conservative and Reform, between Bar and Bat (and Bas) Mitzvah, between chazzan and shammes and gabbai (I had a rough, if somewhat skewed, notion of what a rabbi was.)

Which brings me to the real purpose of this preface, the acknowledgements. These questions of mine—along with hundreds of others that I formulated as I worked my way downstream from the headwaters of Congregation Neveh Shalom—had to be answered. Some were answered by my own reading; some were answered by Rabbi Joshua Stampfer, who initiated this project and whose support throughout has been unstinting; but the vast majority of the questions have been answered by the man whose name appears on the title page of this book along with mine—David Bernstein.

One of the few things I know about David besides his dogged determination as a researcher and his unfailing patience with my ignorance, is that he is a competitive swimmer with the Mt. Hood Masters. This strikes me as wholly appropriate, since one of David's repeated tasks as we traveled downstream in our literary raft was to swim ashore and gather provisions while I sat in the stern and scribbled a draft of whatever chapter I happened to be on. How or where David found these provisions—what archival underbrush he had to whack through, what territorial creatures he had to contend with—are matters that remain mysterious. What I do know is that David would always catch up with me a mile or so downstream with the needed material in hand, looking hardly the worse for wear. His contributions to this history—especially to the early years, his area of special interest and expertise—constitute a service to Congregation Neveh Shalom that rivals that of officer or benefactor—a legacy of knowledge for future generations of Jews.

While acknowledging David's invaluable contributions, however, I hasten to add that ultimate decisions about what to include or exclude have been mine, not David's. In particular, I finally decided to leave out a number of individual family histories that David took considerable pains to collect and that congregants were kind enough

Preface

to supply. In one or two instances, I overrode David's advice in favor of a principle my father ingrained in me: "When in doubt, use your own poor judgment." In each instance, my own poor judgement was to sacrifice sometimes interesting and hard-sought material to what I perceived as the integrity of the narrative.

Consequently, a good portion of thanks must go to people whose contributions are only meagerly reflected in the text that follows. These include, for starters, all those volunteers who were eager to help but were never called upon, largely because of my meager managerial skills: Delphine Davis, Sadie Feves, M'Liss Gilbert, Frieda Tobin, Judy Weinsoft, and Rose Zidell. In this category must also go various former presidents who graciously supplied detailed summaries of their administrations, much of which information did not find its way into the book: Allan Sherman, Al Feves, Norman Wapnick, Mark Ail, Hershal Tanzer, and Richard Brownstein. Once having made the decision to follow a thematic rather than a chronological approach to the final chapter, into which most of this material would have gone, I found that many details of these various summaries were simply unsuitable. Again, my thanks to these would-be contributors, and my apologies.

Lest all of this create the impression that David and I produced this book double-handedly, however, let us acknowledge some of the many people whose help was indispensable.

- The Neveh Shalom 120th Anniversary Committee, who decided in favor of this project and who supported its progress: Karen Berman, David Bernstein, Arnold Cogan, Sheri Cordova, Norman Eder, Julie Gottlieb, Rennee Holzman, Al Horwitz, Carol Koranda, Toinette Menashe, Marcy Morris, Ron Morris, Darlene Pope, Cantor Linda Shivers, Rabbi Joshua Stampfer, Paula Stewart, Hershal Tanzer, Roberta Taskar, and Idelle Weinstein.

- Stella Klebe, whose generous donation made the publication of this book possible.

- The researchers, who performed the tedious task of reviewing and abstracting hundreds of pages of minutes, congregational bulletins, Portland Jewish newspapers, and photo collections that were the building blocks of this book: Annette Charack, Gussie Cooper, Hilde Jacob, Donna Jackson, Al

Koplan, Paul Lavender, Mose Lindau, Sandra Oster, Helen Saperstein, Dave Sims, and David Spigal. Also, Norton Stern of the *Western States Jewish History* magazine, who researched early histories recorded in San Francisco and other out-of-town newspapers.

■ Lora Meyer, who served as research consultant and who provided material from the files of the Jewish Historical Society of Oregon.

■ Adolph Asher, Irma Banasky, Esther Feldstein, Suzanne Itkin, Heinz Jacob, Dorothy Kohanski, Sally and Hedwig Scheuer, and Marcia Weinsoft, who shared their personal or family memoirs with us, and Abraham "English" Rosenberg, who proved an invaluable source of information about Congregation Neveh Zedek.

■ Sandi Rosenfeld and Leah Rubin, who supplied material on the United Synagogue Youth and the Foundation School respectively, and Esther Menashe and Carol Rotstein, who supplied material on the Sisterhood.

■ The members of the High School Project of 1984, whose account of the 1961 merger supplied much valuable material on that period of Neveh Shalom history.

■ Al Horwitz, who did an outstanding job of collecting and editing the photographs, and Bill Vertrees, who made all the arrangements for the printing of this publication.

■ Sheri Cordova, who performed numerous administrative tasks; Roz Newhouse, who transcribed various tapes; My Fowler, who entered the entire manuscript into computer; Sandy Axel, who helped with graphics; Martie Sucec, who sized the photos; and Louis Pain, who proofread the manuscript.

■ The reviewers, who saved the author much embarrassment by catching oversights and offering thoughtful suggestions: Elaine Cogan, Toinette Menashe, Lora Meyer, Goldie Stampfer, Rabbi Joshua Stampfer, and Shirley Tanzer.

Preface

■ Henny Bernstein and Patty Cassidy, who tolerated and encouraged their respective husbands over many months, and Nicolas Cassidy Miranda, who did without his "Papa" on many occasions with all the grace that an eight-year-old can muster.

And, no doubt, others whom we have overlooked with no intention of offense.

That the book itself may cause unintended offense to some is, it seems to me, inevitable. The interwoven histories of Neveh Shalom, Ahavai Sholom, and Neveh Zedek are cross-stitched with squabbles over matters great and small, and I would be surprised if this history did not lend itself to that well-grounded tradition. In particular, former Neveh Zedek members are likely to feel—with some justification—that material about their long-loved congregation is overshadowed by the space devoted to the history of Ahavai Sholom. To point out that there are reasons for this—including the paucity of written records from Neveh Zedek—is not likely to soften the perceived slight. To put a matter out of your mind is not to put it out of your feelings.

But the interwoven histories that follow reveal yet another consistent trait of the congregations in question—namely, the ability to set aside personal differences in the face of great crises or on occasions of great joy. The celebration of which this book constitutes a modest part is without question such an occasion. Marking as it does an anniversary of 120 years, it is an occasion both unlikely and illustrative. As the history of the Jewish people has proven again and again, the odds against survival are always impressive, but not nearly so impressive as the spirit by which they are overcome. This book is a tribute to that spirit.

1869-1891
How We Got Here

*The ocean is where we come from.
Rivers are how we got here.*
—David Quammen

The dictionary defines *congregation* as "a body of assembled people." In reality, however, a congregation is more like a body of water, and most like a river: moving and changing, expanding and receding, accumulating force as it goes. The headwaters of the river may be accessible, but even these owe their existence to changeable forces that are merely more remote. To tell the story of a congregation, then, is like entering a river. You choose a spot, and you step in.

We step into our story in the 1850s, the decade that saw the first influx of Jews to Oregon. By any standard, the 1850s were a remarkable period in American history, marked by such great technological advances as the railroad and the transcontinental telegraph and such literary masterpieces as *Moby Dick, Leaves of Grass,* and *Walden.* Despite the mounting tension over the slavery question, the predominant mood of the country was one of optimism and adventure, a mood reinforced by the recent discovery of gold in California. That not everyone shared the general enthusiasm about "progress," however, is evident from the following passage from Henry David Thoreau's *Walden*, published in 1854:

> One says to me, "I wonder that you do not lay up money; you love to travel; you might take the [railroad] cars and go to Fitchburg

to-day and see the country." But I am wiser than that. I have learned that the swiftest traveller is he that goes afoot. I say to my friend, Suppose we try who will get there first. The distance is thirty miles; the fare ninety cents. That is almost a day's wages.... Well, I start now on foot, and get there before night.... You will in the meanwhile have earned your fare, and arrive there sometime to-morrow, or possibly this evening, if you are lucky enough to get a job in season. Instead of going to Fitchburg, you will be working here the greater part of the day. And so, if the railroad reached round the world, I think that I should keep ahead of you....

Thoreau's complaint about the railroad and his defense of the paradox that "the swiftest traveller is he that goes afoot" is a charming and, some would say, totally impractical argument against progress. What Thoreau is really giving us here is a parable, one that might serve as a starting point for a history of Congregation Neveh Shalom.

Like Thoreau, the founders of the synagogue that was to become Neveh Shalom had two main reservations about modern "improvements"—that they went too fast, and that the price they exacted was out of proportion to their advantages. In the case of the founders of Ahavai Sholom, the improvements in question were not technological, but ritualistic. Those who were originally members of the Reform Temple Beth Israel, founded in 1858, felt that the traditional practices to which they were accustomed were being abandoned with too great haste and at too great a cost—namely, their sense of Jewish identity.

The resulting conflict was not untypical of Jewish congregations throughout the country at that time. Such Reform innovations as the abolition of certain parts of the worship service, the introduction of mixed choirs, and the revision or abandonment of the accustomed prayer books were common causes of dissension. Bitter dispute over the modernization of the Jewish religion was, by the 1860s, the order of the day. What is important to keep in mind is that behind the disputes was a common goal: the preservation of a treasured religion in a changing world. As with Thoreau and his friend on their way to Fitchburg, the argument was not about where to go to, but about how to get there.

1869–1891 / How We Got Here

A bout the same time that Thoreau was writing, Oregon was witnessing the first influx of Jews from San Francisco, the East, and Europe—most notably from southern Germany. According to census reports, the population of Jews in Oregon grew from one in 1850 to 100 in 1860, and about half of that latter number resided in Portland.

The first Jews to arrive in Portland found a frontier town of 600 people housed in wooden buildings that lined muddy, stump-filled streets. (The stumps were white-washed so that pedestrians wouldn't bump into them at night.) Still, the beginnings of the city-to-be were visible. Churches, stores, and a school had been built, and a weekly newspaper was in the offing.

The Headwaters: Germany and Prussia

Front and Stark Streets in 1852. Courtesy, Oregon Historical Society (OHS).

Most of the early arrivals were single men, itinerant peddlers in search of a place to sell their wares from a wagon or, with luck, to open a store. Those who settled tended to do so tentatively and in the downtown area, living above their places of employment. Typical were the first two whom we know by name, Jacob Goldsmith and Lewis May, who ran a general merchandise store on Front Street for a couple of years and then left. But other Jews kept coming, and by 1853 the town census recorded 19 Jews. By far the majority of these were originally from rural towns in southern Germany. Even as late as 1860, the census lists three-fourths of the city's Jews as being from south Germany, with only 13 percent from Prussia and four percent from Poland or Russia.

As depressing as Portland's wet climate may have been to these early German immigrants, it was obviously preferable to the depressed economic climate of central Europe. Moreover, except during the short-lived relief that accompanied the reign of Napoleon, to be a Jew in Bavaria during the first half of the nineteenth century meant to be the object of discriminatory restrictions that affected both business and family life. In 1813 an edict was passed that limited the size of Jewish families and the kinds of occupations that Jews could pursue. When Napoleon became a name revered by Jews throughout Europe for convoking the first Great Sanhedrin in eighteen hundred years, the future of the German Jews suddenly brightened. But Napoleon's military defeat at Waterloo, sealed by the Congress of Vienna in 1815, snuffed the candle of Jewish hopes and returned the old order. Nor could the ill-fated revolts of 1820, 1830, and 1848 rekindle the flame. If anything, the plight of the German Jews was even more bleak, for they had, however briefly, seen how the world looked by the light of civil liberties. Many of them set out to find that spark again, this time in America.

But to many of the Jews who arrived in New York and other large East Coast cities in the early 1850s, the land of opportunity must have seemed only slightly less crowded than the ships on which they had made their long and arduous transatlantic crossing. Nor did it take many of them long to catch the echo of "Go west, young man!" that had heralded the rush to California after the discovery of gold at Sutter's Mill in 1849. Despite the promise of transportation miracles implicit in the burgeoning railroad, "rush" was still a relative term in the 1850s. But west they went, to seek their livelihoods if not their fortunes.

On the West Coast, however, the German Jews found their skills more suited to selling than mining, and as California failed to pan out for the vast majority of miners, a number of the immigrant Jews followed the trail of abandoned gold towns to Oregon. By 1858 enough of them had arrived in Portland to feel the need for a congregation. And so on June 13 of that year, after much discussion, Congregation Beth Israel was founded. Just over a decade later, it would be from this congregation that, amidst mounting dissension between the traditional and Reform factions, four of the eight founders of Ahavai Sholom would defect.

1869–1891 / How We Got Here

Though we have scant information about the founders of Ahavai Sholom, we know that the federal census listed their birthplace as "Prussia." Later, after the unification of Germany in 1871, the distinction between southern German and Prussian-Polish Jews becomes more difficult to determine, since increasing numbers of Jews from what had been Prussia/Poland began identifying their birthplace as "Germany." But the distinction was not lost on the Eastern European Jews who began to arrive in the 1880s and who referred to Beth Israel as the "Deutschesha shul," (German synagogue) and to Ahavai Sholom as the "Polisha shul" (Polish synagogue). Moreover, this distinction played a significant role in the formation of the congregation whose history this book celebrates.

The designation "Prussian" has a special meaning in Western Jewish history. Prussia, the dominant state in pre-unification Germany, was located primarily in the eastern part of the country, with scattered holdings as far west as the Rhine River. The western provinces of Prussia contained few Jews, but to the east lay the former Grand Duchy of Posen and other Polish territories that Prussia had acquired in 1793 when the Polish kingdom was divided

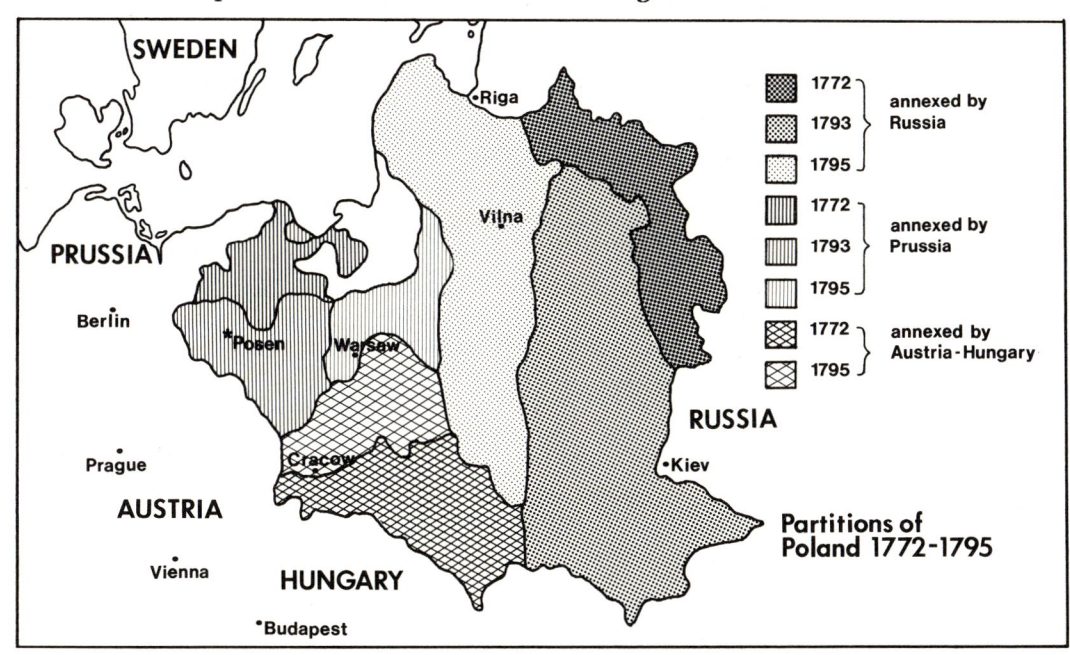

The partitions of Poland, showing the areas annexed by Russia, Prussia, and Austria. All but one of the founders of Ahavai Sholom were Prussian Jews from the region of Posen. Courtesy, Sandy Axel.

11

for the second time between Russia and Prussia. Posen alone, from which most of the founders of Ahavai Sholom came, accounted for two-fifths of the entire population of Prussian Jews.

As the part of independent Poland nearest to the west, the Duchy of Posen had experienced the influence of German culture even before the partition, so that the transition to Western culture had progressed considerably by the time Posen joined Prussia. The Prussian schoolmasters had thoroughly grounded the Posen youths in the principles of the German Enlightenment (*Aufklarung* in German, *Haskalah* in Hebrew), central to which was establishing German as the primary language in place of either Polish or Yiddish. When Moses Mendelssohn (1729-1786) translated the Pentateuch into German, written in Hebrew characters, he had rightly surmised that the Jews would use his translation as a bridge to the larger world of German secular literature and science. Even for Poseners who did not pursue an advanced education, their knowledge of German later allowed them to interact with German Jews in America, while their religious training constituted an equally strong link with the masses of immigrants from Russian Poland and Russia—two factors that would play an important part in the history of Congregation Ahavai Sholom.

But almost as fast as the Poseners could be transformed into Prussians and acculturated to the German language, they began to emigrate. The partition of Poland had brought the problems of Eastern Europe to the forefront, and the Posener Jews were quick to intuit trouble ahead. *"Die Not is nach Schwersenz gekommen"*— "Schwersenz (a community in Posen) is in for dire straits"— was a proverb of the day. In the span of 40 years, between 1831 and 1871, the Jewish population of Schwersenz shrank from 1,603 to 72, mostly as a result of emigration to the United States. "Nowhere else that Jews live," reported the *Algemeine Zeitung des Judentums* in 1851, "produced such a significant immigration to America as the Grand Duchy of Posen." A smaller number of Poseners emigrated to England first and then to America, acquiring a knowledge of English on the way.

The Poseners differed from the German Jewish immigrants in that they were usually artisan tailors rather than peddlers. Even those who followed the lure of the Gold Rush often began in the mining camps as tailors. They differed also in that they were far less susceptible to the forms of the Reform movement, which had originated in Germany. Thus, both in major cities such as New York,

Chicago, and Cincinnati, and in smaller Jewish communities similar to Portland, it was not uncommon to find parallel congregations of Germans and Poseners. In many cases, this phenomenon was the result of reluctance on the part of the Poseners to abandon the Polish rite of prayer, but, as we shall see, this seems not to have been the case in Portland.

Realizing that the Poseners would eventually comprise a significant part of American Jewry, the Reform movement made considerable effort to induce them to abandon their traditional conservatism. One tactic was to publish accounts of how well the Reform was doing in Posen itself, thus appealing to the Posener's pride in his homeland. Such propaganda was only moderately successful, however, and for several decades Posener congregations in America remained the backbone of religious conservatism. As Rudolf Glanz puts it: "Changes in services and rites of the Posener congregations appeared only gradually, and often after in-fighting. If such a congregation became Reform it was followed in many cases by secession and the formation of a new conservative congregation." And on this score, Portland was no exception.

Separate Ways: The Split from Beth Israel

It was from Prussia, then, that the founders of Ahavai Sholom came, mostly from the province of Posen. Arriving in Portland, they found a city that was beginning to shed its frontier character. It was, after all, the second largest city on the West Coast and the Pacific Northwest's leading commercial and financial center. It was steadily building a manufacturing base, not only in lumber but in other consumer goods. Though its main links with the outside world were the ships that came up the Columbia River, Portland was already linked by rail to Forest Grove in the west and Albany in the south. The city boasted 22 hotels, and though none of them had first-class accommodations, the city directory could proudly proclaim that "Portland has ceased to be an experiment."

But the Poseners also found a city of approximately 460 Jews and only one synagogue, Beth Israel, which had not quite ceased to be an experiment. The ongoing experiment was a transition from traditional German to American-type Reform practices, and every change was the subject of bitter dispute. Rabbi Julius Eckman, Beth Israel's first rabbi, had left in 1865, unable to abide the changes the congregation was implementing. The hiring of Rabbi Isaac Schwab in 1867 failed to moderate the factional disputes. His re-election

Following A River

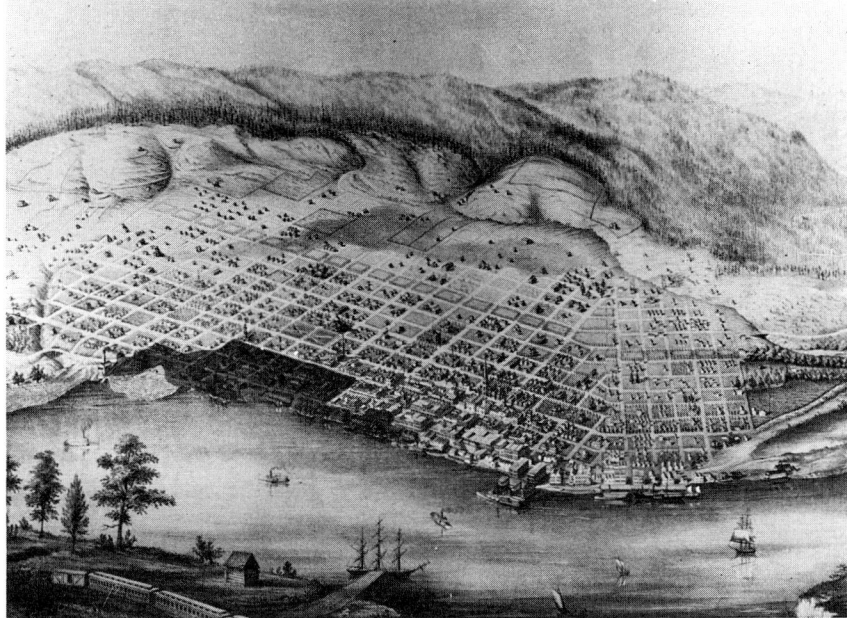

An artist's aerial view of Portland in 1870, a year after the founding of Ahavai Sholom. Courtesy, OHS.

amidst a storm of controversy in 1869 seemed to bring matters to a head for those Prussian-Polish Jews who were the most resistant to the Americanizing of Judaism. A group of them decided to leave Beth Israel and join a group of unaffiliated Jews in forming a new congregation. We have no way of knowing how many of each element made up the initial membership of the new congregation, but of the eight original officers and trustees, four were former members of Beth Israel and four were apparently unaffiliated.

Nor, really, do we have any way to determine exactly what motivated the formation of a new congregation. On the basis of circumstantial evidence, however, we can at least question two of the more commonly proposed conjectures. One is that the reasons were largely financial—specifically, that the cost of membership at Beth Israel was too high. This reason is first mentioned in an article in Portland's Jewish Newspaper, the *American Hebrew News*, for December 24, 1897, which notes that "a few of the new settlers in Portland, who had applied for pews to the officers of the other congregation [Beth Israel] and were exacted to pay an amount beyond their means...determined to have a congregation of their own, no matter how modest." While we can hardly disregard such an explicit statement in one of the earliest sources available, we should also keep in mind that within a relatively short time the new congregation would purchase a cemetery and a city lot, build a synagogue, and hire one of the West Coast's leading rabbis. While far from being the "merchant princes" that were later to emerge from Beth Israel, the founders of Ahavai Sholom were small business men ready and able to take on substantial financial obligations. Money may certainly have been a factor in their defection from Beth Israel, but it was not likely the major one.

The second reason commonly put forth for the Prussian-Polish defection from Beth Israel was that the Poseners preferred to use the ritual they had used in the Old Country, the Minhag Polen. This scenario parallels the situation in San Francisco, where the Polish Synagogue Sherith Israel and the German Emanu-El, each using its own national ritual, were organized almost simultaneously in 1851. In point of fact, however, Ahavai Sholom adopted the Minhag Ashkenaz, or German ritual, that was used at Beth Israel. Ironically, twenty years later in 1889, the constitution of the "Polish synagogue" still specified the traditional German ritual, while the "German synagogue" of Beth Israel had abandoned it.

But while the difference between German and Polish ritual may not have been a factor, we can hardly assume that the almost exclusive Prussian-Polish make-up of the new congregation was mere coincidence. One of the strongest—one might almost say most hysterical—statements about the rift between the German and Polish Jews that contributed to the respective make-up of the two congregations appears in the San Francisco *Hebrew Observer* some five months after the founding of Ahavai Sholom:

> Albeit that the Jews [in Portland] are *ostensibly* divided owing to a different mode of worship; the one [Ahavai Sholom] congregation being orthodox. . .while the other [Beth Israel] is reform. . .I perceive that the division is based upon a more serious groundwork, vis: the sin that one portion of the Israelites here have committed in having seen the light of the world for the first time in another country than the other party has. . . Where will you find Catholics or Protestants, or people of any other denomination despise one another because they happened to have been born a few miles further north or south? Deny it as we may, this sad state of affairs exists here, and may God avert the evil that such an unheard of prejudice may produce. [Note: in this and other early sources, the term "orthodox" is used to designate any synagogue that is not Reform, since the term "Conservative" was not yet in common use.]

"Despise" and "prejudice" are strong words, perhaps stronger than the situation merited. Still, Jewish archivist Scott Cline points out that "the Germans believed they were culturally superior to the religiously conservative Poles, and the latter often fed that belief." In support of this, Cline cites a rather poignant recollection of Polish-Jewish author Harriet Lane Levy of San Francisco:

> That the Baiern [Bavarians] were superior to us, we knew. We took our position as the denominator takes its stand under the horizontal line. "Polack" confessed second class. Why Poles lacked the virtue of Bavarians I did not understand, though I observed that to others the inferiority was as obvious as it was to us that our ashman and butcher were of poorer grade than we, because they were ashman and butcher.

However vehemently the San Francisco Jewish press may have viewed the situation, this polarization between Polish and German Jews was not as pronounced in Portland as it was in San Francisco. Nor had Portland class consciousness reached the point that it would two decades later, when the German Jewish elite would institutionalize the division between German and Pole with the creation of the exclusive Concordia Club. Still, if such a division existed in Beth Israel in 1869, one can well imagine the Polish Jews' frustration at being considered denominators to the German numerators.

Nor, finally, should we let considerations of national origin exclude the possibility of mere personality clash. One of the dangers of reconstructing histories on the basis of constitutions, census records, and city directories is forgetting that we are not talking about statistics, but about people—in this case, about two relatively small groups of earnest individuals who, despite sharing a common religion, may simply have not liked each other.

Founders and Foundations

Newman Goodman, President; Leiser Cohn, Vice-President; Phillip Levin, Secretary; Raphael Prag, Treasurer; Jacob Batt, Marx Franklin, Charles Goldstein, Joseph Harris, Trustees: after all the conjectures about motivation, we are left with the concrete fact of these eight names on the incorporation papers of Chevra (Society) Ahavai Sholom. The names of other members referred to as "founders" appear in subsequent records, but their status can't be verified. Moreover, only the last name and first initial of these eight men appear on the papers, removing their humanity even further from our curious gaze; the first names were obtained from the federal census. And since any personal records that these eight men may have left have never been located, it is to the federal census and the Portland City Directory that we must again turn to reconstruct a profile of them and their families.

The typical founder was 35 to 45 years old and married to a woman seven to 10 years younger. In almost every case, both husband and wife acknowledged "Prussia" as their birthplace. The men were in either the dry goods or produce business on Front or First Street, then the commercial center of the city. The family had four or five children, had previously lived in California, and had come to Oregon about 1865.

Into these dry facts we can blend the rather moist prose of one "Judeus," the Oregon correspondent for the San Francisco *Hebrew*

Front Street as shown in an 1888 publication.. Several founders of Ahavai Sholom located their businesses here. G. Cohn & Bro.," right foreground, was the family business of Leiser Cohn, a founder of Ahavai Sholom. The Esmond Hotel stands on the site where the first services of the soon-to-be congregation were held in 1866. Courtesy, OHS.

Observer, who writes in 1869 that "the mass [of Jewish men in Portland] are given to trade (and we know no instance of a parent having had the ambition to make him devote his son to any of the professions, nor the solid sense to devote him to the less precarious vocation of the mechanic)." It is worth noting as a sign of the times that "parent" here is synonymous with "father." As for the mothers, Judeus goes on to describe them as "thrifty and active housewives," and the daughters as "more truly womanly, more simple, hence happier and healthier than the wire puppets in the larger cities."

None of the current families of Neveh Shalom can trace its roots back to any of the founders of Ahavai Sholom. Newman Goodman, Ahavai Sholom's first president, left the congregation he had helped form and rejoined Temple Beth Israel. His granddaughter, Gladys Goodman Trachtenburg, and her son John are current members of the Temple. The Harris and Prag families still have members living in the Portland area, but none is of the Jewish faith. These latter founders, incidentally, are the only two whose graves can be found in the Ahavai Sholom cemetery, though we have reason to believe that two others, Leiser Cohn and Joseph Batt, may be buried in unmarked graves. All of the remaining three died, left town, or left the synagogue within 10 years of its founding. These facts alone would lend credence to an observation made in the *American Hebrew News* article already cited—namely, that "for some time the members had a hard struggle to maintain the congregation."

Leiser Cohn, second president of Ahavai Sholom. This is the only known likeness of a founder. Courtesy, OHS.

The year 1873 seems to have been a particularly hard one for the founders and their families. Piecing together scraps from various sources, we find that this was the year in which Charles Goldstein left town, Phillip Levin's dry goods business on First Street was destroyed by fire, Newman Goodman resigned his presidency and possibly returned to Beth Israel, and Jacob Batt fell or jumped into the Willamette River and was drowned. According to an article in the *Oregonian*, Batt's body was recovered at Willamette Falls in Oregon City, and while the exact circumstances of his death are not reported, it is noted that he had tried to commit suicide the previous summer by cutting his throat. The article also mentions that the body was turned over to L. Cohn, President of Ahavai Sholom synagogue,

1869–1891 / How We Got Here

and that it was buried at "a Hebrew cemetery south of Portland"—presumably Ahavai Sholom, though, as we have noted before, no record or grave marker has been found.

The prompt acquisition of a burial site was a prime consideration among Jews in the pioneer West. A Jewish burial was almost universally desired, even among those who had been unobservant during their lives. In California gold rush towns, for example, Jewish cemeteries were established even though there was never an organized congregation. In Ahavai Sholom's case, the need for a cemetery possibly had political overtones as well. Mt. Zion cemetery, which had been formed in 1856, had been taken over by Beth Israel in 1862. Without a cemetery of its own, Ahavai Sholom would not only have been at a disadvantage in recruiting new members, but would have been in the uncomfortable position of having to petition the rival synagogue for places to bury its dead.

And so it was that on June 3, 1869, two days before the formal incorporation of Ahavai Sholom, five of the original members of the fledgling congregation purchased a five-acre tract of land in Multnomah County from a farmer named J. M. Tice. (Tice had originally obtained the land from the federal government as part of the Donation Land Claim, an earlier version of the Homestead Act, which provided free land to settlers.) Eight days after the five members purchased the property, they resold it to the congregation for the original purchase price. The deed to the property describes the land as being reachable by "Old Milwaukie Road" from "Boon Ferry Road." At the time, the property was connected to the main route only by an unimproved road, but it is indeed the site of the present-day Ahavai Sholom cemetery.

The cemetery is the only tangible legacy handed down from the founders. To walk through it today, noting the juxtaposition of old and new, ornate and plain, is to be reminded of the dynamic tension between the past and the future that runs like a cross-current through the history of Congregation Neveh Shalom.

One of the oldest tombstones in Ahavai Sholom cemetery, marking the burial site of founder Raphael Prag and his family. Courtesy, Neveh Shalom (NS).

19

A Man and A Place: Rabbi Julius Eckman

A portion of the Hebrews in Portland, Oregon have found it necessary to form themselves into a congregation and extend to us an invitation to take abode among them. We shall leave with the steamer next Tuesday, please God, and expect to find matters at our place of destination agreeably to expectations; our stay there may be a prolonged one.

So wrote Julius Eckman, the soon-to-be first rabbi of Ahavai Sholom, in a letter of August 20, 1869. Sixty-four years old when he penned these optimistic lines, Eckman was hardly a naive, young rabbi. Nor was he unfamiliar with the politically sensitive situation in Portland to which he was returning. He had originally come to Portland in 1863, leaving the editorship of the San Francisco *Weekly Gleaner*, to serve as the first rabbi of Beth Israel. As already noted, however, he left after two years amidst considerable conflict with the young congregation, and returned to San Francisco to take up the editorship of the the *Hebrew Observer*. On September 17, 1869, the latter paper approvingly cited an editorial from the New York *Hebrew Leader*, which noted that Ahavai Sholom's choice of its first rabbi was "a very happy one, as Rev. Eckman possesses all the qualities required to act in a conciliatory spirit, and especially to reconcile in love and peace the different views entertained by the members of the congregation." Even more pointedly, the editorial goes on to say:

> We sincerely rejoice at the circumstance that the Portland congregation does not follow destructive tendencies, which only produce chism [sic] in Judaism. It is to be regretted that there are congregations to be found which adopt the said destructive tendencies, without being aware of their inevitable results, through the influence of the idle talk of unscrupulous Reverends, who palmed the same upon them as true Judaism.

In short, the Reverend Doctor had his work cut out for him, and he knew it. But Julius Eckman was no ordinary man, and no stranger to work. His career as a journalist, educator, and fund-raiser had made him a prominent public figure in San Francisco and, as the New York paper's editorial suggests, even beyond. On his departure from San Francisco, the *San Francisco Call* described him, definitively, as "one of the best men that ever lived in San Francisco." The *Examiner* was hardly less enthusiastic. Noting that Eckman had been given a going-away present of a purse filled with a large amount of

1869–1891 / How We Got Here

Julius Eckman, Ahavai Sholom's first rabbi. In his biography of Eckman, Pioneer Rabbi of the West, *Rabbi Joshua Stampfer observes: "Rabbi Eckman epitomized the spirit of the West with his vigor, his curiosity, his creativity. He reflected the task that lay ahead for generations of American Jews—to embrace change while maintaining a firm grasp of the Jewish heritage." Courtesy, Laurie Levich.*

gold, and that he had turned over the entire amount to a committee for the relief of suffering in Prussia and Russia, the *Examiner* exclaimed, in upper-case letters, "THAT'S THE MAN FOR US."

Apparently, the founders of Ahavai Sholom shared this sentiment, though for different reasons. The same firm position that had eventually alienated Eckman from the membership of Beth Israel—preserving the traditional aspects of Judaism while permitting only modest reforms—recommended him to the founders of Ahavai Sholom. Moreover, he was one of them, having been born in 1805 in Rawicz, a city in Posen. And so, after purchasing the cemetery site and, on June 8, 1869, incorporating the congregation, they lost no time in tending to the next order of business: securing a religious leader who would add credibility and stature to their enterprise. We can only assume that they were delighted when Eckman agreed to accept their offer.

In the meantime, though, they needed a place of worship. The first services of what was to become Chevra Ahavai Sholom had been held in 1866 at a location at Front and Morrison that would later

21

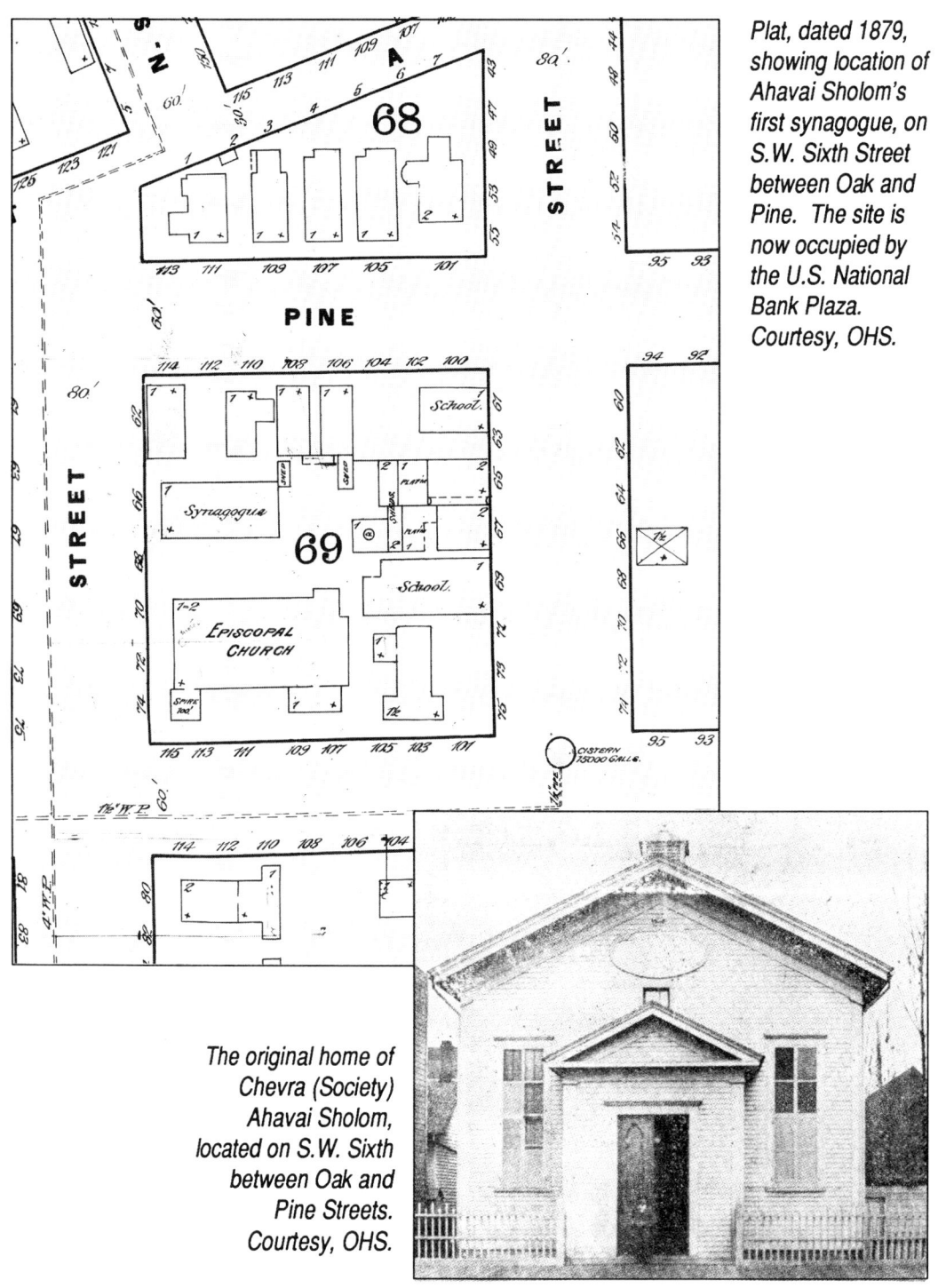

Plat, dated 1879, showing location of Ahavai Sholom's first synagogue, on S.W. Sixth Street between Oak and Pine. The site is now occupied by the U.S. National Bank Plaza. Courtesy, OHS.

The original home of Chevra (Society) Ahavai Sholom, located on S.W. Sixth between Oak and Pine Streets. Courtesy, OHS.

be occupied by the Esmond Hotel. A Dr. Davison of Victoria, B.C. had officiated. Between 1867 and 1868 the services had been held on Stark Street between First and Second, next to the Ladd and Tilton Bank, in a building usually used for "theatrical purposes." Clearly, neither of these places would serve as a permanent sanctuary nor be fitting for the congregation's distinguished first rabbi. And so, again according to the *American Hebrew News* of December 24, 1897, "a lot 25 X 100 on Sixth and Oak was purchased at the price of $1,000." While never the most reliable of sources when it comes to details (the more dependable *Observer* notes that the main hall measured 30 X 50 feet), the *News* goes on to state that "The location, then isolated, is now the center of population, and has in consequence become very valuable property, $22,000 having already been offered for it." (The site is now occupied by the U.S. National Bank Plaza.)

The High Holiday services for 1869 were held not in the new synagogue, but in the Washington Armory, though they were conducted by Rabbi Eckman. A correspondent for the *Oregonian* (the article, reprinted in *the Hebrew Observer* of October 22, 1869, implies in several places that the writer is Roman Catholic) was deeply impressed by the combination of solemnity and simplicity that marked the occasion. Given what we know of Ahavai Sholom's origins, the writer's description of Rabbi Eckman's sermon is of particular interest:

> The preacher earnestly impressed it upon the minds of his congregation not to allow themselves to be carried away by the spirit of the age (by rationalism) which, instead of converting souls to religion, betrays the soul to the world, and, being worldly, is so pleased with the world, which it mistakes for religion, that it congratulates itself at the religion it has found at last (its own reason deified) and calls it—reform!

As we know, Rabbi Eckman had good reason to want to underscore the conservative bent of his newly-formed congregation.

Sometime between October and December of 1869 the new synagogue was completed, since the formal dedication took place on December 5 of that year, a Sunday. Close to 300 people, both Jew and Gentile, attended, including such honored guests as Major General George Crook, Henry Failing, W. S. Ladd, and former Governor A. J. Gibbs. The *Observer* supplies us with a contemporary account of the ceremony:

Following A River

> While the choir was singing "How Goodly Are Thy Tents, O Jacob," Rabbi Eckman entered the sanctuary holding a Torah scroll and ascended the pulpit. He explained to all present, making special mention of the Gentiles present, that the Torah was the focal point of Jewish life throughout the years of the Diaspora. He then marched about the synagogue seven times, followed by the offerers, explaining that by this ancient custom they were making the synagogue the center of their life. He pointed out that the number seven in its Hebrew roots was related to the words for plenty, vows, and worship. The scrolls were then placed in the ark and the dedication service continued. The invited dignitaries, the congregational offerers and Rabbi Eckman, all contributed their share to the heart moving exercises. Everyone was particularly impressed that such a small and young congregation could have built such a handsome structure.

The *Observer* also supplies us with an excellent description of the interior of the "handsome structure," which, coupled with surviving photographs of the exterior, allows us to reconstruct the synagogue that would serve as Ahavai Sholom's place of worship for the next 35 years:

> The main hall measured thirty by fifty feet and was provided with pews that would seat two hundred people. Each pew was furnished with a bookshelf and a footstool. There were several pendant chandeliers, each with double rows of gas burners. There were in all thirty-four gas jets, enough to light the room brilliantly. The walls were hard finished and the general aspect of the room was exceedingly cheerful. The altar and pulpit were made of handsome walnut. The altar was draped with purple and gold silk.
>
> Over the entrance was a small semi-circular gallery for the choir, capable of seating about eight people. Over the ark was placed the Hebrew Ten Commandments carved in wood. The schoolroom at the rear of the synagogue proper measured 20 X 30 feet and was capable of accommodating sixty to seventy students. The average attendance of the Sabbath school was about a hundred so they had to use the main sanctuary as well.

The emphasis on religious education of the young, charmingly suggested by this picture of children overflowing from the schoolroom into the main sanctuary, was to become one of the hallmarks of Rabbi Eckman's tenure at Ahavai Sholom. "The teaching of

1869–1891 / How We Got Here

children," along with the promulgation of the Jewish faith and the burying of the dead, had been one of the explicit purposes stated in the papers of incorporation, and the establishment of a school had been one of Rabbi Eckman's first acts upon assuming leadership of the congregation. While his powers as a preacher inspired the new congregation and his reputation as a scholar drew the attention of the entire community, it was his obvious affection and interest that attracted the children. He, in turn, found the religious nurturing of these young minds one of the chief joys of his calling.

Rabbi Eckman's stay in Portland was not as "prolonged" as he had anticipated, for he remained at Ahavai Sholom for only three years. During that time, however, the congregation took this kindly, scholarly man to their hearts. But the pace of duties and the longing to retire among his many close friends in San Francisco became too much for the aging rabbi. His last recorded act as rabbi, noted in the Multnomah County marriage register, was to officiate at the wedding of Anna Harris, daughter of founder Joseph Harris, and one Simon Stone, in November of 1872. His leave-taking from Portland was tinged with sadness on both sides, and his going-away present on this occasion was not a purse of gold, but a beautiful Kiddush cup, inscribed "From your children."

As we have already noted, 1873 was an especially difficult year for Congregation Ahavai Sholom. How much this can be attributed to the departure of Julius Eckman in the previous year is impossible to say, but the sense of loss must have been great. One small but touching evidence of this is the fact that, in 1875, Newman Goodman, having resigned his presidency of Ahavai Sholom and returned to Beth Israel, named his newborn son Jules Eckman Goodman. The good rabbi was gone, but he was hardly forgotten.

1873–1884: The "Lost" Years

T he decade following Rabbi Eckman's departure from Ahavai Sholom offers a stark contrast to its widely publicized beginnings. During these years there is practically no mention of the congregation in either the Jewish or the secular press. Nor are there many internal sources to consult, since all of the congregational minutes up to 1884 were lost in a fire. Referring to this period, a short history of the congregation published on the occasion of its 70th birthday in 1939 observes that "The earlier history [of Ahavai Sholom] is found in oral records, transmitted from father to son." We no longer have access to such records, of course, any more than mothers or daughters seemed to have had access to them in 1939.

Of the rabbis who served the congregation during this period, therefore, we have little information, in some cases only names. For example, the article in the *American Hebrew News* of December 1897, already noted for its lack of accuracy on detail, refers to a Rabbi "Arago." The Portland City Directory of 1876 does list a "Rev. S. Arager, Rabbi" as living on S.W. Sixth between Washington and Stark, about a block away from the synagogue. Presumably, this is the same man, though whether or for how long he served as rabbi to Ahavai Sholom we have no way of knowing.

Another obscure name—that of Herman Bories—appears on a marriage certificate of 1879 as "Minister acting for Cngr. Ahabai Sholome [sic]." Bories, a Bohemian-born shoe dealer and educated layman, had served as teacher and sometime chazzan for Beth Israel in the early 1860s. How much religious leadership he exercised at Ahavai Sholom is not known, though as late as 1890 he requested that he be appointed assistant rabbi "for the purpose only of marrying couples."

Of Rev. Marcus Mellis, who served as rabbi from 1880 to his death in 1882, we have only slightly more information, though we do know a good deal about his sons. They operated a wholesale and retail dry goods business, Mellis Bros. and Co., with retail stores in Portland and Oakland, California, and a buying office in San Francisco (David Solis-Cohen, later to become a prominent figure in the Portland Jewish community, was a partner.) In 1883, a year after Rabbi Mellis' death, a commercial magazine described the buying office as being four stories and rivaling anything in San Francisco. By 1885, however, the business had disappeared from the City Directory altogether, and two of the sons, Frederick and Theo, are listed in different businesses. Theo continued to be associated with Ahavai Sholom as a Sunday School teacher until his departure to Baker, Oregon, in 1888.

As for Rabbi Mellis himself, most of our information comes from an article in the *American Israelite* in December of 1882. Like most of the articles in the *Israelite* during this period, this one is characterized by unabashed bias and tortuously long sentences. It does manage to inform us, however, that Rabbi Mellis was "for many years rabbi of small towns and congregations in Bohemia (Austria) and for the last three years minister of the strictly Polish and decidedly orthodox congregation Ohavai Sholom [sic] of this city."

The same sentence goes on to mention Mellis' learning in Talmudic lore, and ends by characterizing him as a "fanatic" if amiable old gentleman whose idiosyncrasies should be forgiven. The members of Mellis' family, understandably not sharing the writer's reservations, erected an impressive marble gravestone in the shape of a pulpit with an open book on top. Mellis' two sons, neither of whom married, are buried on either side of him.

The grave marker of Marcus (Mordecai) Mellis, rabbi of Ahavai Sholom from 1880 to 1882. Courtesy, NS. Translation, Rabbi Joshua Stampfer.

This grave marker provides an example of an acrostic tombstone inscription, a fairly common practice of the times. The first letters of each line in the Hebrew inscription spell out the deceased's given name, "Mordecai." An English translation reads:

M *You were a faithful guide to your people*
R *The high qualities of the Torah you revealed (to them)*
D *Know Daughter of Zion! Lover of Peace and Life*
C *Your waves are as a mighty sea. But do not despair*
AI *He will seek good for you. Also in the heights of heaven*
   He will be your spokesman forever, Mordecai the Jew!

(The final line is an allusion to Mellis' family name, Melitz—that is, "spokesman.")

Finally, we come to a man who, appropriately, closes the "lost years" of Congregation Ahavai Sholom: Rev. Robert Abrahamson. Abrahamson first came to Portland in 1880, and served as cantor when Marcus Mellis was still rabbi of Ahavai Sholom. He had been trained in Frankfurt-on-the-Oder, Germany, and had assumed his first pulpit in Brandenberg, Prussia, in 1868. After coming to America in 1872, he spent the next eight years with congregations in New

Following A River

Rev. Robert Abrahamson. While not formally ordained, he served Ahavai Sholom alternately as cantor and rabbi for almost 40 years. Courtesy, NS.

Jersey and Georgia. After Rabbi Mellis died in 1882, Abrahamson remained at Ahavai Sholom for two more years, long enough to earn a place in the congregation's affection. In 1884 he resigned and, for the next two years, traveled in Europe, the West Indies, and South America. As we shall see, this short period of his absence marked one of the most hectic in the synagogue's early history. Fortunately, Rabbi Abrahamson would return in 1886, this time to begin a spiritual and financial renewal that would take the congregation through most of the next 35 years.

For Lack of A Leader

When the congregation surfaces from this period of obscurity in the first surviving minutes of 1884, it does so as a religious community struggling to stay afloat. The enrollment had dwindled to 35 members, and the departure of Rabbi Abrahamson had left the small group with neither rabbi nor chazzan to lead them in services. The minutes are peppered with complaints about the condition of the cemetery, noting several occasions on which the funeral home had threatened not to conduct a funeral there if something wasn't done. The only note of optimism was sounded by an advertisement for a new leader that appeared in several Jewish newspapers in June of 1884. The ad specified that congregation Ahavai Sholom desired "the services of a competent chazzan who is able to officiate with a choir, who also possesses the capacity of mohel and shochat and ability to instruct in Hebrew and religious school." To expect all this for a "fixed salary, $900 per year plus $300 in perquisites, no travel expenses" required a genuine leap of faith.

The fiascoes that followed on the heels of this ad are worth recounting, partly as evidence of the obstacles that the congregation had to hurdle and partly in contrast to the exemplary leaders whom we shall see later. One of the respondents to the June ad was I. Kaiser of Denver, Colorado, who was invited to officiate at the High Holidays and, in the following October, accepted a contract. Within three months, however, the minutes disclose that the congregation

1869–1891 / How We Got Here

Copy of the earliest surviving minutes of Congregation Ahavai Sholom, dated May 25th, 1884. The minutes of Congregation Neveh Zedek have not been preserved. Courtesy, NS.

had become "cognizant of the fact of Mr. Kaiser having acted morally in a manner unbecoming of a teacher of children," and that a committee had been appointed to inform him of the "fact of its being the desire of the congregation that he resign." Three days later the trustees were informed by Mr. Kaiser that he was resigning "because of ill health and the necessity of a change of climate as ordered by the physician." Ironically, had the fire that destroyed the congregation minutes occurred just a year later than it did, our only record of Kaiser's departure would have been this brief notice in the *American Israelite:* "The congregation Ahavai Sholom has suffered a loss. The chazzan who became so popular, and who took unto himself a fair helpmate from our midst has sent in his resignation and gone to California to try the effect of a change of climate. The congregation accepted the resignation with regret...."!

Undaunted by their experience with Kaiser, the trustees placed a second ad and, by the end of February, had a second chazzan. This was a Rev. G. A. Danziger (no relation to Henry Danziger, who faithfully served as the congregation's president from 1884 to 1890), 27 years old, from Vincennes, Indiana. Wary after the unseemly departure of Mr. Kaiser, a committee had examined Danziger's credentials and found him a satisfactory candidate, skilled at lecturing in both English and German. But again, disillusionment set in early. By June, the Rev. Mr. Danziger was charged with "conduct unbecoming a minister," and was suspended. A law suit over back pay ensued, but was thrown out of court a year later by one Judge Shattuck. Again the report in the *American Israelite* is one-sided, noting only that "Rabbi G. O. Danciger [sic] explains he is leaving Ahavai Sholom because they have not paid in 3 1/2 months."

All of this, as indecorous as it may seem, ultimately redounds to the credit of the still young congregation. Despite their dwindling attendance at services (by 1886 things were so bad that President Danziger "advised the closing up of the synagogue" because of the "general neglect of divine worship by the members," and moved that any member not attending service at least once a month be fined $1.00), despite their occasionally unfortunate choice of leaders, they persevered. They were being tried in the furnace of affliction, and their ability to come out only slightly singed speaks strongly in their favor. For this too, perhaps, some of the credit must go to Julius Eckman, who had given them such a high standard of what a true spiritual leader should be, and to Robert Abrahamson, who had held out the hope that such a standard could indeed be met and who would return to fulfill that hope.

In the meantime, however, the High Holidays of 1885 were approaching and the congregation had no one to lead services. But their luck, it seems, was starting to turn. Somehow, for the modest fee of $150 and no travel expenses, they managed to contract one of the most outstanding Jewish religious leaders of the pioneer West, Abraham W. Edelman of Los Angeles. Born in Poland, Edelman had gone to San Francisco in 1859 and then to Los Angeles in 1862. Fluent in Spanish, Hebrew, English, and German, Edelman was apparently never formally ordained. Still, the congregation that he served for many years, B'nai B'rith, conferred on him the title of Rabbi and still acknowledges him as its first spiritual leader. Congregation B'nai B'rith is now known as Wilshire Boulevard Temple and, besides being the oldest Jewish synagogue in Los Angeles, is one of the largest and most influential Reform congregations in the West.

As it turned out, Edelman just happened to have been retired by B'nai B'rith when the call came from the small, remote outpost of Judaism in Oregon. Despite a number of relatively "reform" changes that he had introduced, he was apparently too "old school" for a congregation striving for social prominence. Consequently, not being ready for retirement, he actively sought the post in Portland.

Rabbi Edelman arrived in June of 1885 and conducted the High Holiday services that fall. He apparently made a good impression, since he was offered and accepted a contract as "reader" for one year. December of 1885 finds him officiating at Ahavai Sholom and reorganizing the Shabbat school. On January 8, 1886, the Oregon correspondent for the *American Israelite*, who by now was beginning to sound like a baseball sportscaster announcing relief pitchers for a losing team, declared that "the orthodox Congregation Ohabe Sholom [sic] has at last succeeded in electing an honorable gentleman as their chazzan and we fervently hope that Mr. Edelman, formerly of Los Angeles, will be better than his predecessor." (This latter jab is most likely a reference to the ill-fated Mr. Danziger, though it could also refer to either the "fanatic" Rabbi Mellis or even to Robert Abrahamson: one is hard put to second-guess the tastes of the Oregon correspondent for the *American Israelite!*)

Rabbi Edelman may have been "better," but he was hardly more permanent. He resigned the following June, citing the dampness of the Oregon climate as his reason. One is tempted, perhaps foolishly, to read between the lines here. It may have been that a congregation of some 35 members was simply too small for a prominent rabbi from Los Angeles, or it may have been that the Northwest in the days before rail service was simply too isolated. Money seems not to have been the problem, since Edelman had a good income from astute real estate investments made years before in Los Angeles. The only evidence of internal discord is a cryptic note in the minutes for May 2, 1886, a month before Edelman's resignation: " A motion to dismiss the chazzan was lost." All the other evidence, however, suggests that the congregation was genuinely sorry to lose such a distinguished leader. Still, their newly found good fortune seemed to be holding, for the year of Abraham Edelman's departure also saw the return of Robert Abrahamson, of whom we, too, shall be seeing more later.

A Distant Voice: The 1889 Constitution

In rounding out this sketch of the early years of Ahavai Sholom, we might pause to look at the oldest known copy of the congregation's constitution and by-laws, dated 1889, exactly a hundred years ago. It was placed in the cornerstone of the synagogue's second home, on S.W. Park Street, at the dedication ceremony in 1904. Much of the document covers the routine procedures of any such organization—how officers were elected, how dues and fees were collected, and so forth—many of which are the same as those observed today. A number of the items, however, provide interesting if minor insights into the character of the congregation.

For one thing, the 1889 constitution specifies only three duties of the synagogue: holding services, assisting the sick and needy, and burying the dead. The section headed "Object of the Society" makes no mention of the education of the young, which had been specified in the incorporation papers and had been so important to Julius Eckman. This is a curious oversight, especially in view of the fact that the January 6 minutes of 1889 talk of building a new synagogue for the express purpose of providng "a separate school large enough to hold twice as many students." Given the previous and subsequent history of Ahavai Sholom, one is inclined to assume that religious education was so obviously a priority that the drafters of the constitution didn't feel obliged to mention it.

Equally curious at first glance is the fact that the position of rabbi is nowhere described or required. The constitution specifies only that a "minister or chazzan" is to be elected, and describes his duties (including the duty "to kill poultry at the request of a member of the society without remuneration"—a stipulation that hints at an historical struggle between chazzan and congregation over this source of income.) This failure to mention a rabbi may, of course, reflect the congregation's less than outstanding success in attracting seminary-trained spiritual leaders after Rabbi Eckman's departure in 1872.

Other noteworthy items in the 1889 constitution deal with features of synagogue life that are taken for granted today. It is specified, for example, that the books and proceedings be kept in

CONSTITUTION.

ARTICLE I.
NAME OF THE SOCIETY.
This society shall be known by the name of "CHEBRA AHAWAI SHOLOM."

ARTICLE II.
OBJECT OF THE SOCIETY.
The object of this society shall be to keep divine services on every Sabbath and Holiday; to assist the sick and needy and perform all duties to a deceased member and his family as may be designated in the By-Laws hereafter.

ARTICLE III.
LANGUAGE.
The proceedings and books of the society shall be kept in the English language.

ARTICLE IV.
OFFICERS AND THEIR ELECTIONS.
SECTION 1. The officers of this society shall consist of a President, Vice President, Secretary, Treasurer, four Trustees, a Visiting Sick Committee and Messenger. They shall be elected annually by the members of the society.

SEC. 2. The nomination and election shall take place at the meeting in October and the installation in November.

SEC. 3. All candidates for office must be members in good standing, whose membership shall have been at least three months in the society, and must be able to read and write the English language.

First page from Ahavai Sholom's 1889 constitution. Note Article III, which specifies English as the official language. Courtesy, NS.

English and that the officers and trustees be able to read and write in English. Also, the by-laws place what might strike us as excessive emphasis on maintaining decorum during services, a duty for which both the president and the trustees are held responsible. These provisions, however, reflect a time when German was still the dominant language in many congregations and when, as we shall see in the next chapter, the arrival of Eastern European Jews was beginning to make orderly services a controversial issue.

Finally, the by-laws regarding membership reveal a screening process that was fairly rigorous. Potential members are required to have been residents of Oregon or Portland for at least three months, and blackballing is provided for. The latter was done literally—that is, a black ball could be placed in a ballot box, and five black balls would reject a candidate for membership. Once accepted, members could bid annually for assigned seats, the remaining unsold seats being available to members for $2.50 and to non-members for $5.00. Failure to attend services at least once a month resulted in a fine, though how or whether this was enforced is left to our imaginations.

To our imaginations as well is left the task of translating these formal by-laws and trivial minutes into an impression of the actual people whose lives and hopes they reflect. Occasionally a universally human chord is struck and we succeed, as when the minutes of May 23, 1889, express "condolence to our noble president on the drowning death of his son Moses Danziger." For the most part, though, our imaginations fall short of the task. Later, when the history of the congregation begins to take on the accents of human voices that we recognize or even remember today, the task will be easier. But the voices we hear now are muffled by a hundred years of static. Even so, if we listen carefully, we can recognize them as the voices of Jews who, despite the hard times they have come through, are eagerly discussing plans for a new synagogue, plans for a larger school, plans for the future.

1892-1922
Respecting the Past

*We must respect the past, remembering
that once it was all that was humanly possible.*
—George Santayana

Mergers and Muddy Waters

So far we have been exploring the headwaters of one tributary of the congregation whose 120th anniversary this book is celebrating. But Congregation Neveh Shalom has another tributary whose headwaters are, if not as old, at least as remote as those of Ahavai Sholom—namely, Congregation Neveh Zedek Talmud Torah, more commonly referred to as Neveh Zedek. As most of us know, Neveh Zedek and Ahavai Sholom merged in 1961, becoming the present-day Neveh Shalom. What is less well-known is that the two congregations had previously merged and, after a stormy year, separated again—and this before the turn of the century.

"The President here stated that he called this special meeting for the purpose of considering the communication received from Cong. Novah Zedik [sic] regarding amalgamation." This brief note, buried in the minutes of Ahavai Sholom for November 12, 1895, is remarkable for two reasons. First, it places the founding of Neveh Zedek at least five years earlier than is generally assumed. Second, it refers to an attempted "amalgamation" between the predominantly middle-of-the-road conservative Prussian-Polish Jews of Ahavai Sholom and the more recent arrivals from various parts of the Russian Empire, who tended more toward orthodoxy. To understand the outcome of that attempt, we need to review the national origin and religious background of the Russian immigrants who founded Neveh Zedek.

Unlike the Prussian Jews, whose main motivation for emigration was economic, the Jews from Eastern Europe were the victims of outright persecution. Though Catherine the Great of Russia had attempted, in 1762, to make all of Russia off-limits to Jews, the three partitions of Poland (1772, 1773, and 1795) had foiled her plan by placing 900,000 more Jews under her rule. Still, these Jews were largely restricted to the territory along Russia's western border known as the Pale of Settlement. By 1850 the Pale had shrunk to about half its original size, and most Jews lived in the shadow of starvation, despair, and possible violence. The bizarre and ill-fated reign of Alexander II offered a brief period of liberalism and hope, but this was cruelly shattered on March 1, 1881, by an assassin's homemade bomb. When the dust had settled, Russia was under the rule of Alexander III, whose answer to the "Jewish question" would become "one-third conversion, one-third emigration, and one-third starvation." The pogroms (Russian for "like thunder") that he encouraged between 1881 and 1884 echoed throughout the world, bringing storms of protest at the calculated massacre of thousands of Jews. In 1882 the infamous May Laws were passed, further restricting the movement of Jews and ultimately leading to the expulsion of Jews from many areas. Some help came from voluntary Jewish relief organizations in Europe and America, but for hundreds of thousands the only hope lay in emigration to the United States, whose immigration laws were as yet unrestricted.

The Russian Jews who eventually arrived in Oregon brought with them a firm loyalty to old ways, both in their religious rituals and in community values, combined with a fierce sense of self-determination. Unlike most of the German Jews, who had originally come to Portland as single males, the Russian Jews arrived in families, which partly accounts for their tendency to stick together rather than mix physically and socially with their new Gentile neighbors. To the resident Jews, who by now were a stable element in Portland society, the newcomers seemed unreasonably clannish with their "backward" ways and strange language. Determined to preserve the family and communal values that had helped them survive in the Old Country, the Eastern European Jews gravitated to South Portland, where housing was relatively cheap. They formed there what amounted to a Jewish "ghetto" with a lively and colorful culture all its own. Geographically, the area ran north and south from Harrison to Whiteaker Streets, and east and west from the Willamette River to about Broadway.

It was from this background and environment that the founders of Portland's first Russian congregation emerged. Here, however, the headwaters get muddy. We are relatively certain that in 1902 two Russian congregations, Neveh Zedek and Talmud Torah, joined forces to become Neveh Zedek Talmud Torah. We also have fairly reliable evidence that one of these, Chevrah Talmud Torah, was formed in 1893 for the purpose of instructing Jewish children in Jewish history and the study of Hebrew. (An article in the *Jewish Tribune* of June 19, 1908, places the founding of Talmud Torah in "the latter part of the '80s," and the merger with Neveh Zedek in 1898, but the article later contradicts even itself about these dates.) As for Neveh Zedek, what little contemporary literature there is on this subject places the beginnings of that congregation at the turn of the century, seven years after the founding of Talmud Torah. Prompted by the discovered reference to Neveh Zedek in the 1895 minutes of Congregation Ahavai Sholom, however, further research turned up a brief notice in the *American Hebrew News* of December 24, 1897, referring to Rev. J. Blaustein, then chazzan of Ahavai Sholom, and to his "coming to Portland from the East to take charge of the congregation Novah Zedeck [sic]" in the year 1892. Based on this finding, it would seem that Neveh Zedek, not Talmud Torah, was the first Russian congregation in Portland.

More interesting than this chronological quagmire, however, is a question that it inevitably raises. If there were already two Russian congregations in Portland in 1895, why did one of them—Neveh Zedek—seek to merge with Ahavai Sholom rather than with its Russian counterpart, Talmud Torah? As far as we can reconstruct the situation, the reasons were largely financial. Specifically, the minutes of Ahavai Sholom strongly suggest that the merger was the result of a particular set of financial circumstances that resulted in the second departure of Rev. Abrahamson.

The year preceding the merger with Neveh Zedek—1894—was something of a traumatic one for congregation Ahavai Sholom, marked symbolically by the passing of the last surviving founding father, Joseph Harris, and by the great flood of that year, which rendered their synagogue unserviceable. More significantly, the congregation was also in deep water financially, though in this, too, they were hardly alone. The major depression of 1893 had left 500 banks and 15,000 businesses in bankruptcy nationwide and, having

Following A River

a major effect on the railroads in the Northwest, left its mark on Portland as well. The minutes of Ahavai Sholom reflect the strain. In October of that year, the services of an organist were dispensed with "because of the condition of the Congregation's finances." A month later a "special meeting regarding finances" was held. The minutes

The great flood of 1894 as seen from S.W. Sixth Street. Ahavai Sholom Synagogue is in the center, between a hardware store and an Episcopal church. Courtesy, OHS.

note that "After hearing the object of the meeting, Rev. Abrahamson stated he was willing to give up $12.50 of his normal $112.50 monthly salary." Subsequent events suggest that "the object of the meeting" may have indeed been to cut Rev. Abrahamson's salary, perhaps by more than he was willing to "give up." When, in November of 1894, Abrahamson's contract was renewed for another three years, the congregation might well have wondered how they were going to afford even the reduced amount, since the minutes show the chazzan's salary accounting for roughly three-fourths of the year's total expenditures, leaving "cash on hand" at only $336.36.

But their worries on that score were premature. In December of 1894, a month after the renewal of his contract, Abrahamson withdrew his application, stating that "I have reason to believe since I have sent my application it does not seem to meet with harmonious consideration that it is for the best interests of the future prosperity of your congregation." "Prosperity" seems to be the key word here, though the phrasing of "your congregation" hints at some serious discord that is surprising, given Abrahamson's years of amiable association with Ahavai Sholom and the honored status that he attained in his later years with the congregation. Whatever the reasons, Abrahamson had decided to leave Portland and take a pulpit in Seattle, and the only question that remained was whether he would officiate for the High Holidays of 1895. In July of that year, he said that he would not. Apparently aggravated, the board withheld the usual letter of recommendation given to a departing minister. The whole affair seems to have been an unfortunate mess, resulting in, among other things, the resignation of the president, Meyer Raphael, in September of 1895.

Meanwhile, Congregation Neveh Zedek must have been in at least as dire straits financially, and probably more so. It was a much younger congregation and, given its origins, probably had fewer members of social or financial prominence. What it did have, however, was a chazzan, Rev. Jacob Blaustein, whom the *American Hebrew News* described as "a fine Hebrew scholar and a thorough Talmudist" with "a musical voice. . .and a good musical education." A surviving photograph reveals a young man (he was 32 when he came to Portland in 1892) with considerable presence and a hint of professional ambition. He and his congregation may have seen the departure of Rev. Abrahamson from Ahavai Sholom as an opportunity to merge with a more established synagogue, while Ahavai Sholom probably saw Blaustein as the answer to their problem of not

Following A River

Cantor Jacob Blaustein. Blaustein went from Neveh Zedek to Ahavai Sholom during the brief merger in 1895 and returned to Neveh Zedek in 1898. Courtesy, OHS.

having a chazzan for the High Holidays. A condition of the proposed merger was that Blaustein should retain his office of chazzan for at least one year. When, in November of 1895, Ahavai Sholom accepted the proposal (by a vote of 13 to six), Blaustein was given an 18-month contract originally stipulating a monthly salary of $75. This was later changed to $50, exactly half of what the departing Abrahamson had been receiving. Interestly, the *American Hebrew News*, while not mentioning figures, notes that when the two congregations merged, Blaustein was retained as chazzan *"with an increase of salary."*

In theory, everyone stood to benefit from the merger, and the *American Hebrew News* predicted a happy union despite "all factional considerations and what slight differences of religious opinions that hitherto separated them." An incipient sore point, however, seems to have been that, in contrast to the later merger in 1961, Neveh Zedek lost both its identity and its assets: three Torah scrolls, furniture, and their cemetery areas, all of which became the property of Ahavai Sholom. Moreover, the 22 former members of the Russian Neveh Zedek were now members of Ahavai Sholom, whose form of worship was the German ritual of Minhag Ashkenaz. Adding to the potential for discord may have been the fierce sense of independence that characterized Neveh Zedek right up until the successful merger in 1961.

Whatever the reasons, some of the former Neveh Zedek members were unhappy with the arrangement and, in May of 1896, withdrew from the new congregation on the grounds of "dissatisfaction as to the mode of worship." In July, only seven months after the merger, eight of the departing members requested the return of Neveh Zedek property, apparently with the aim of reestablishing the congregation. The matter was complicated, however, by the fact that not only Blaustein but a significant number of former Neveh Zedek members chose to remain in their new congregation. In the election of October 1896, the president-elect, Isaac Apple, the vice-president, and several of the trustees were all former Neveh Zedek members. (Apple's election was unusual both in that it was contested and that the first ballot found him in a 17-17 tie with a former president, Meyer Raphael. A second ballot, for which one of the Raphael supporters was absent, left Apple the winner in a contest that may well have been along factional lines. Apple, however, never finished his term, resigning in March of 1897—when he was replaced by Raphael—and a month later leaving the congregation altogether. He was later to be president of Neveh Zedek, thus becoming the only person to serve as president of both Ahavai Sholom and Neveh Zedek.)

As with many floundering relationships, a period of what pyschologists call "denial" seems to have set in by early 1897. During the same March meeting at which Isaac Apple resigned, another request for a settlement with Neveh Zedek was tabled on the grounds of the congregation's "not being aware of the existence of a Congregation Novah Zedek [sic]." In April, Ahavai Sholom received another request from the "newly organized" Neveh Zedek, which was also tabled. Finally, in May of 1898, Ahavai Sholom faced reality and voted to turn over some books and bookcases to the "new" congregation, thus acknowledging that the union was over.

In July of 1898, within a year of the dissolution of the merger, Jacob Blaustein was asked to resign his post with Ahavai Sholom and returned to become chazzan of Neveh Zedek, which was to merge with Congregation Talmud Torah in 1902, the same year that saw the founding of the more strictly "orthodox" Shaarie Torah. (The ad to replace Blaustein at Ahavai Sholom called for someone who could "act as chazzan according to the orthodox ritual," though again this most likely reflects nothing more than the broad use of the term "orthodox" to refer to any non-Reform synagogue. As late as 1920, an article in the *Scribe*—the Jewish community's "Record of Jewish Life and Thought" that ran from 1919 to 1953—refers to Congregation Neveh Zedek Talmud Torah as "orthodox," even though other evidence precludes the reference being understood in the modern sense.) The first rabbi to serve Talmud Torah and then the newly formed Neveh Zedek Talmud Torah was Nehemiah Mosessohn, a member of the family that published Portland's *Jewish Tribune*. Mosessohn left within a year, however, as did his successor,

Rabbi Adolph Abbey. The only clue to the reason for Abbey's departure is a brief statement in the 1911 congregation history, which notes that in 1904 the congregation was "divided because of rabbi." Whatever the reason, about half of the congregation left at the same time, presumably to join Shaarie Torah. Though Neveh Zedek's next rabbi, Henry Heller, would remain for four years—from 1907 to 1911—it is clear that Ahavai Sholom was not the only Portland congregation that had trouble retaining spiritual leaders.

A month after Jacob Blaustein left Ahavai Sholom, Robert Abrahamson returned from Seattle to once again become chazzan of Ahavai Sholom, where he remained the rest of his life. It was almost as if the merger between Neveh Zedek and Ahavai Sholom had never happened, which is indeed how subsequent chroniclers treated it. The next 65 years were to witness two more proposed or attempted consolidations between the two congregations before they successfully merged in 1961 as Congregation Neveh Shalom. History, famous for repeating itself, occasionally gets it right.

An ad from the American Hebrew News of 1898, reflecting the needs of the three congregations that would eventually become Neveh Shalom. At the time of the ad, Cantor Jacob Blaustein had returned to "Novah Zedech," and Rev. Robert Abrahamson was about to return to "Ahavia Sholom." Courtesy, Jewish Historical Society of Oregon (JHSO).

CONGREGATION TALMUD TORAH,
ROSH HOSHONAH AND YOMKIPPUR.
Services Sixth and Hall Streets

All persons wishing seats for the coming Holidays can procure tickets at the Synagogue, Sixth and Hall streets every Sunday from 9 to 12 a. m. DURING THE WEEK tickets can be had from S. KAFKA, First and Madison streets

Congregation Ahavia Sholom.

Seats for the coming Holidays will be sold at the Vestry on Sixth Street, between Oak and Pine, Commencing Sunday morning, August 21st, at 10 o'clock, and every Sunday following.

S. H. ABRAHAM, 387 Taylor St.,
J. DELLER, 1st & Yamhil,   } Committee.
J. ASHER, 1st & Salmon,

Congregation Novah Zedech.

The Congregation Novah Zedeck will hold services on Rosh Hashonah and Yom Kippur at the A. O. U. W. hall.

The competent rabbi, Rev. J. Blaustein will officiate with a choir. If you want to enjoy a pleasant holiday and hear a fine musical chasan, then you are invited to attend.

We hope and trust that all who appreciate his fine musical talent will attend. Tickets will be sold at a reasonable price. Tickets can be obtained by M. Hochfeld, 193 Front street, near Taylor; I. Friedman, 293 First and Columbia; S. Hochfeld, 265 Front street, between Madison and Jefferson.

Officers as Leaders: A Tale of Two Isaacs

According to *The American Hebrew News*, both the idea and the "successful accomplishment" of the 1895 merger were the work of two officers of Ahavai Sholom, President Isaac Gevurtz and Secretary Isaac Swett. So far, we have been directing much of our attention to the spiritual leaders of Congregation Ahavai Sholom, somewhat at the expense of its officers. The names of the congregation's presidents—Goodman, Danziger, Raphael, and Apple—have caught our eye intermittently, but mostly as background scenery intended to orient us to the main action. The list of presidents in the appendix to this book underscores that the period we have just been discussing was one of extreme instability in the congregation's leadership. In the nine-year period from 1884, the year of the first recorded minutes, to 1893, only three men served as president; the next five years saw eight changes in the presidency, including one person elected who resigned before taking office. Throughout this turmoil, as the recurrence of certain names on the list indicates, the burden of leadership tended to fall to a few individuals, of whom Gevurtz and Swett are preeminent examples. Moreover, with these two men we can emerge for the first time from the shadowy world of congregational minutes and occasional newspaper articles into the earshot of human voices. Both men's lives are documented and both can be recalled by people living today. In the case of Gevurtz, his descendants are still active in the congregation to the present day.

Unlike the Posners who founded congregation Ahavai Sholom, both Swett and Gevurtz were from Russia, which may in part account for their interest in negotiating the merger with their fellow Russian Jews of Neveh Zedek. Isaac Swett arrived from Odessa in the Ukraine in 1882 with his father, Leon. The elder Swett had been strongly influenced by the *Am Olam* movement, which advocated a return to the soil as the means of revitalizing the Jewish spirit. Attracted to New Odessa, an idealistic agricultural colony in Roseburg, Oregon, Leon Swett nevertheless decided to put the practical matters of raising his family above his own idealistic leanings, and purchased a small berry farm in Buxton, northwest of Portland. To his son Isaac he bequeathed both his intellectual curiosity and his love of the land.

The merger with Neveh Zedek was clearly not the only thing on Isaac Swett's mind in 1895, for he was also finishing law school, from which he graduated the following year. A letter of Swett's dated 1897 presents a young man with a clear sense of personal values: "I am no

Isaac Swett. Rural pioneer, active Zionist, and lawyer, Swett was a dynamic presence both as secretary of Ahavai Sholom and as a leader in the B'nai B'rith movement. Courtesy, JHSO.

Early presidents of the National Council of Jewish Women, including Julia Swett, far right. Like her husband, Isaac, Julia Swett was a prominent force in the Jewish community, succeeding him as executive secretary of the Federated Jewish Societies. Courtesy, JHSO.

less a farmer for being a lawyer.... The money to go to university I made on the farm, my vacations are spent working on [the] farm, and [I] now practice in winter months in Portland and farm the rest of the year. Indeed, my love for the soil is so strong that even when practicing I board out of town about three miles, where there is a little land I can work at, morning and evening." Both his education and his devotion to farming contributed to Swett's later important role in the Zionist movement, one goal of which was to revitalize traditional agricultural values.

As a lawyer and as an officer of Ahavai Sholom, Isaac Swett was strong-minded, outspoken, and eloquent. All of these qualities are reflected in a surviving photograph, which shows him with his back to the camera and his head turned in a dramatic profile. Besides using his considerable gifts in the service of Ahavai Sholom, he became one of the founding members of Sabato Morais Lodge 464 of B'nai B'rith in 1897, just as later he would be on the founding board of the B'nai B'rith Building Association.

Swett is remembered most clearly, however, for his untiring legal work on behalf of the needy and underprivileged. David Spigal, a current member of Neveh Shalom, recalls that when his parents died in Eugene within 26 hours of each other during the 1918 influenza epidemic, it was Swett who came from Portland to look after the three orphaned children. Swett found the children—two boys and a girl—at the home of Esy Rubenstein, founder of the furniture store that still bears his name, and made arrangements for their care until they could be adopted. Coincidentally, Swett and his wife, Julia, also had a daughter and two sons, the youngest of whom, Meyer, had been killed in his teens in an automobile accident on the way to Seattle. Julia Swett, a trained social worker, was also active in children's causes, serving as liaison between the Jewish Shelter Home and the juvenile courts in custody and adoption cases. She was also a force in establishing public kindergartens in Portland and, when Isaac Swett died, she succeeded him as executive secretary of the Federated Jewish Societies. These are just a few examples of why even today the name of Swett is remembered with affection and respect.

Unlike Swett and the majority of the Russian Jews, who arrived after the 1880s, Isaac Gevurtz came to America in the late 1860s. After a short stay in New York and while still a teenager, he established himself in the cigar manufacturing business in San Francisco, only to be wiped out by the panic of 1873. In 1881, after he and his first wife

Isaac Gevurtz. Gevurtz was noted for wearing a "yarmulka" to his furniture store at First and Yamhill, though he insisted that the reason was more practical than devotional: he wanted to keep his head warm in the poorly heated building. Courtesy, Gevurtz family.

The Gevurtz family. Back row, from left: Alec, Philip, Mae (Philip's wife), and Matthew. Middle row, from left: Isaac, Lillian, Fannie, Cacelie, and Louis. The two boys in front are (from left) Harry and Milton. Courtesy, Gevurtz family.

were divorced in San Francisco, Gevurtz took his three small sons and sailed to Portland. There, he opened the first Gevurtz furniture store at Front and Yamhill. The company is still in existence and, unlike other local Jewish mercantile empires such as Meier and Frank that have been absorbed by large corporations, is still a family-run business.

In the early days, Gevurtz did most of his business with the money-shy farmers of the Tualatin Valley, often on the basis of barter rather than cash. In this, he was carrying on something of a family tradition from the Old Country, since his father, an unofficial religious teacher in Lublin, had accepted food and clothing rather than money in payment for his teaching of Hebrew and the Torah. Similarly, the Tualatin farmers would bring in milk, meat, and produce in exchange for furniture, clothing, and stoves, and Gevurtz would keep what food he needed and sell the rest.

Later, when the store moved to First and Yamhill, Gevurtz began to do more business with Portlanders and was one of the first merchants to extend credit, using the slogan "A Dollar Down and A Dollar A Week." One of his ads, which featured a pelican with a feather balanced on its beak and bore the caption "A Little Down on A Big Bill," became a Portland classic. The business grew and prospered, and the store moved at least three more times during Gevurtz's lifetime.

In 1886 Gevurtz married Cacelie Gerson, of German origin, with whom he had three sons and two daughters. As the family's economic situation improved, Gevurtz, like many of his peers, sent for his relatives in Europe. He paid the passage to America for three members of his own family and two of his wife's family, setting the men up in business and helping the women find husbands. This same spirit of generosity extended to his work for Ahavai Sholom as well; the congregation minutes note at least two occasions when Gevurtz loaned money to the congregation to help clear their debts. Moreover, he seems to have been the person the congregation turned to for guidance during its ongoing leadership crises. In the turbulent 1893-1898 period, Gevurtz served twice as president, vice-president, and treasurer, and at least once as director of the religious school.

During the latter part of his life, Gevurtz was attracted to Beth Israel by its dynamic young rabbi, Stephen Wise, and became active there. He retained his membership at Ahavai Sholom, however, and is buried in its cemetery. His son Louis, of whom we shall hear more later, also served as president of Ahavai Sholom, and another son, Harry, became president of Beth Israel,

The year of Gevurtz's second and final presidency (1898) seems to have signaled a return to stability in synagogue politics. As we have seen, Rev. Abrahamson returned to stay, and Morris Gilbert, elected president at the end of the year, remained at the helm for the following six years. The congregation's finances were gradually improving, the benches were filled at services, and the religious school was enrolled to capacity. These latter two points, as we shall see, were mixed blessings, but the fact that Ahavai Sholom survived the turbulent 1890s is itself a tribute to officers like Isaac Swett and Isaac Gevurtz.

Growing Pains: The Need for New Homes

By the turn of the century, any lingering bitterness between Ahavai Sholom and Beth Israel over the split that had occurred a generation earlier had been muted by time. Rabbi Stephen Wise of Beth Israel became a regular lecturer on the second day of Ahavai Sholom's Rosh Hashanah services, a day his own Reform synagogue did not observe. When President William McKinley died in September of 1901, the two congregations held a joint service to commemorate this day of national sorrow.

Still, a degree of rivalry persisted, and Ahavai Sholom could not help but be aware that it was failing to keep pace. While Beth Israel had accommodated its growth in 1889 by building an imposing new synagogue at Twelfth Avenue and Main Street, Ahavai Sholom was still housed in the original synagogue building at Sixth and Oak that had served its needs for over thirty years, and the make-up of its downtown neighborhood had changed dramatically. The Sixth and Oak location had become heavily commercialized, making the property there increasingly valuable. On the other hand, the center of the Jewish population had shifted south of downtown to what is now affectionately known as "Old South Portland," the area originally claimed by the Jewish immigrants from eastern Europe. If Ahavai Sholom was to continue to grow, it would have to move; if it wanted to attract new members, it would have to move south.

First, however, it would have to sell its present home, no easy proposition for any family, let alone for an institution organized on democratic principles. In May of 1900, the board was empowered to

1892–1922 / Respecting the Past

sell the the Sixth Street property for "not less than $10,000," appropriate committees were appointed, and the president and secretary were authorized to negotiate with an agent. The following year found the congregation with an agent in hand, the minimum sale price raised to $13,000, and the pressure for more space increasing (the 1902 annual report notes that the congregation is in "good financial condition" but that the "synagogue is too small to handle High Holiday attendance"). By February of 1903 the board had entertained several offers—one of $15,000 from Beth Israel president and prominent businessman Sig Sichel, who would eventually purchase the property—but the president and secretary were told to seek "better offers." In April, a motion was proposed and carried to raise the minimum sale price to $17,500, and the dickering with various parties resumed. Finally, the treasurer, Simon Abrahams, had had enough. In his 1903 annual report to the congregation, he laid all the cards on the table:

> In my opinion, members made a great mistake in not selling this property for $15,000 that was offered at the time [May, 1903], and much worse by tying it up so it could not be sold for less than $17,500. Gentlemen of the Congregation, I beg of you do not be blind to your own interests.... I know there are at least 40 to 50 people knocking at our door for admission but it is too far for them to come down here. We have taken in less for seats this year than last year; and why? Because we have no desirable seats to give them.... I cannot move old members from their seats that they have been sitting in for 15 or 20 years and give them to new members. In place of increasing, we are standing still, or going backward.

This pleading had the desired effect. On December 17, 1903, a committee was authorized to sell the Sixth Street property for not less than $16,000. Four days later it was sold to Sig Sichel for $16,250 with the provision that the congregation be out by March 1, 1904. Now Ahavai Sholom was under the gun to find a new home.

This time the congregation acted with uncharacteristic speed. Committees were appointed to find a suitable location for a new synagogue and to start a building fund. By the end of January 1904, Ahavai Sholom had purchased a property at Park and Clay Streets and had empowered the board to set the construction plans in motion. On February 19, the congregation held a special service of farewell to the Sixth and Oak building that had been their first home. For the next six months, services were held at temporary quarters on

Third Avenue near Harrison while the congregation waited for its new place of worship.

A local architect, one E. Lazarus, submitted a design and, after adjusting it according to the congregation's wishes ("That we have furnace heat instead of steam heat. That windows be with Cathedral tints instead of plain glass. That ceiling be bronzed."), was given the go-ahead for construction. On the 24th of April, 1904, the cornerstone was laid with appropriate pomp. In the cornerstone were placed copies of three Portland newspapers along with local and national Jewish newspapers, the 1899 constitution and by-laws of Ahavai Sholom, and several curious items, including the business cards of two members, S. H. Abrams and Simon Abrahams. Rabbi Stephen Wise of Beth Israel, by now a regular speaker at Ahavai Sholom, delivered the dedicatory sermon.

Nine months later to the day, Rabbi Wise was delivering another sermon, this time to celebrate the actual completion of the synagogue that would be Ahavai Sholom's home for the next 48 years. The occasion was also marked by a characteristically stirring speech by David Solis-Cohen, of whom we shall see more shortly, in which he described Israel as standing "like a rock in the ocean of time with the light of Sinai shining from its topmost peak." But perhaps the most vivid impression of what the new synagogue had cost the

Program for the laying of Ahavai Sholom cornerstone, 1904. Courtesy, NS.

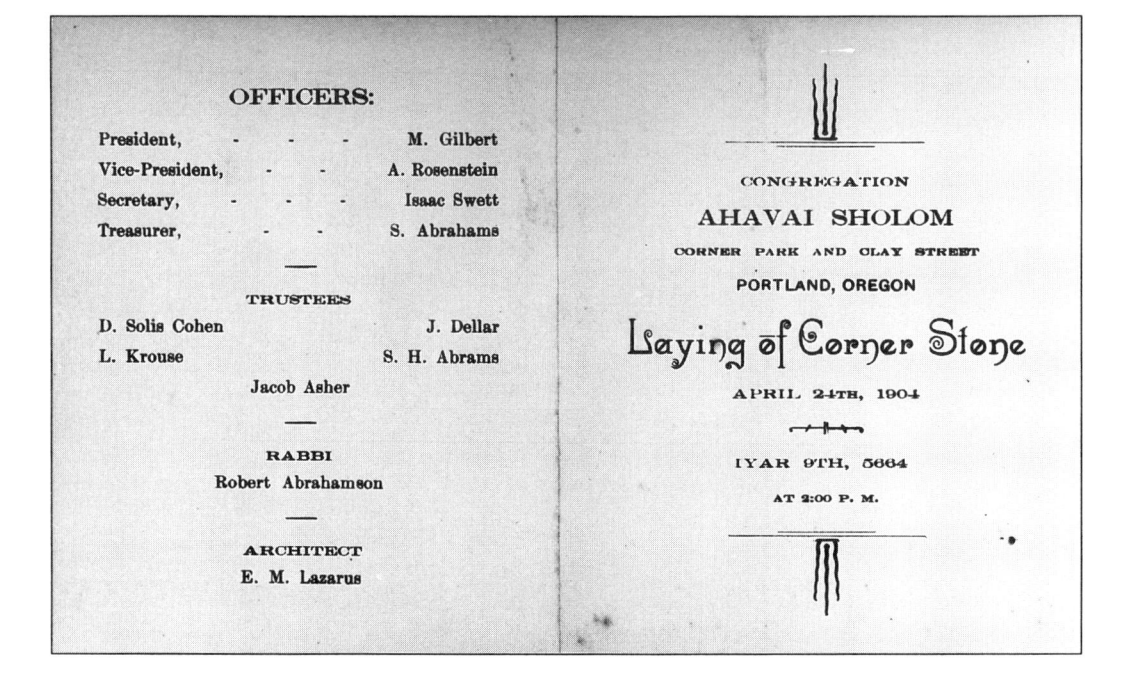

OFFICERS:

President,	M. Gilbert
Vice-President,	A. Rosenstein
Secretary,	Isaac Swett
Treasurer,	S. Abrahams

TRUSTEES

D. Solis Cohen	J. Dellar
L. Krouse	S. H. Abrams
Jacob Asher	

RABBI
Robert Abrahamson

ARCHITECT
E. M. Lazarus

CONGREGATION
AHAVAI SHOLOM
CORNER PARK AND CLAY STREET
PORTLAND, OREGON

Laying of Corner Stone

APRIL 24TH, 1904

IYAR 9TH, 5664

AT 2:00 P. M.

1892–1922 / Respecting the Past

congregation, both financially and emotionally, can be gleaned from the November 6th "president's report" on "the labors of the fiscal year ended." After greeting the congregation with reserve, President Morris Gilbert let out all the stops:

> I can hardly tell you what labors what sacrifices what anxieties this [decision to have a new synagogue] meant.... Our zeal to have a beautiful synagogue almost carried us off our feet. We went to an expense far greater than our most enthusiastic would at first have dared hope.... And here comes perhaps the brightest part of our history; every member was gladly willing to donate far above his means in order that this synagogue be more beautiful. Think of it, our fifty men have contributed twenty-two hundred dollars—an average of about forty-five dollars for each man!
> ... In closing let me say that I have sacrificed my business and often endangered my health in order that our congregation should profit in every way possible, but I feel amply repaid for all I have done in knowing that now we have a Temple that is a credit to everyone of us and to our city—a place that will inspire our children and our children's children. ...May the blessings of God be with this synagogue forevermore.

Morris Gilbert, president of Ahavai Sholom, 1898-1904. Courtesy, OHS.

Having finished what would be his final report to the congregation, Gilbert sat down amidst what must have been the members' universal sense of self-congratulation. And then Isaac Swett, the congregation's firebrand secretary, stood up. " I have little to say concerning all that was done in the past year," Swett began. "The President's report to you...[leaves] nothing to add. I only want to say a few words for the future." Ever the courtroom lawyer, Swett was just warming up.

> We must remember that after all this synagogue was not erected because we could not well worship in the old one but mainly and above all because we thought that a growing Jewish community demanded a beautiful synagogue in a proper location.
> If the old conditions are to continue, if a bare minimum is to

> always be at our services—and this minimum obtained by personal solicitation, if our Sunday School is not to grow in spite of our growing Jewish population, then how justify the sacrifices we have made? Is this to be a beautiful toy? Have we built these walls only to admire them? We must answer these questions and answer them soon.
>
> This congregation has less members than any Jewish congregation in the city, our services are much more poorly attended than any other, our Sunday School has less children than any other Jewish school in town.
>
> These are unpleasant statements—but we are men—and might as well face the truth. But what is worst of all is the fact that there is probably a greater demand for a conservative orthodox congregation like ours than for any other congregation. I believe that there are more Jews in this city favoring a conservative orthodox service than the extreme orthodox or reformed services. In other words, under proper conditions this should be the largest congregation in this city.
>
> I do not underestimate the enormous labors we have performed last year, but I do want to emphatically declare that our work in the future must be greater. . . . Let us be determined to do everything that our place in this community demands.

Swett sat down, perhaps leaving "cathedral tints" on a few faces in the congregation to go with the new synagogue's windows.

Swett's reference here to "extreme orthodox" services was most likely not to Neveh Zedek Talmud Torah, consolidated two years earlier, but to Shaarie Torah, which in 1904 was also in the process of purchasing a a building for a place of worship. Purchased, moved, and ready for services the following year, this building—a former Presbyterian Church—would become the preeminent Orthodox synagogue in South Portland, universally referred to as the "First Street Shul."

As for Neveh Zedek Talmud Torah, it would have to wait until 1911 to dedicate a new synagogue, a much more impressive building than Ahavai Sholom's, with an imposing central tower, beautiful stained-glass windows, and outstanding acoustics. It is from a brief history placed in the cornerstone of this building that we get what sketchy knowledge we have of the early days of Neveh Zedek Talmud Torah. Three names stand out here: Maurice Ostrow, who supplied leadership both as president and as fund-raiser; and the two men who would dominate synagogue politics at Neveh Zedek

1892–1922 / Respecting the Past

for the next three decades—David Nemerovsky and Marcus Gale. For 24 of the 30 years between 1905 and 1935, either Nemerovsky or Gale was president.

One name conspicuously missing from the 1911 cornerstone document is that of Abraham Rosencrantz—and for good reason. In 1911, Rosencrantz, who would very soon become as important to Congregation Neveh Zedek as Robert Abrahamson was to Ahavai Sholom, was still serving as cantor at Shaarie Torah. He had come to Portland from Odessa in 1900, had joined Shaarie Torah in 1908, and would not become cantor at Neveh Zedek until 1915. Once there, however, he remained at Neveh Zedek for the next 21 years, serving alternately as cantor, interim rabbi, and director of religious school activities. But he is perhaps most remembered for his beautiful voice. Frieda Gass Cohen, interviewed in 1975, recalls that her family's house was next door to Cantor Rosencrantz' and that "In the summer we would open our windows and he would open his

Abraham Rosencrantz as a young man in Odessa (left), and as cantor of Neveh Zedek in the late twenties. Though his name is not included in the Neveh Zedek's cornerstone document, Rosencrantz would himself become a cornerstone of that congregation.
Courtesy, NS, OHS.

Ahavai Sholom synagogue on Park Street. This handsome wooden structure would be almost destroyed by fire in 1923. Courtesy, OHS.

Neveh Zedek synagogue, built in 1911. This impressive stone synagogue was one of the finest in the city and a source of great pride to its members. Courtesy, OHS.

History of Congregation Noveh Zedek Talmud Torah from date of organization as Chevra Talmud Torah Sept 12th 1893 to date of laying of the Corner stone of new stone temple.

June 18th 1911.

1893. Chevra Talmud Torah organized. M. Rosenstein President. School and services held above store corner First and Madison Sts.

1894. M. Rosenstein re-elected President. Moved to store room corner 3rd & Mill Sts.

1895. N. Gertzman President. Bought burying ground.

1896. Joe Cohn President. Incorporated as Congregation Talmud Torah and moved to present location 6th & Hall Sts.

1897. M. Simon President. Present premises bought with cash payment of $500.00 and balance of $4000.00 to be paid within ten years.

1898. M. Simon re-elected President.

1899. Wm. Fest elected President.

1900. M. Ostrow elected President. First payment of $200.00 made on $4000.00 note.

1901. M. Ostrow re-elected President. Consolidated with Congregation Noveh Zedek and incorporated as Congregation Noveh Zedek Talmud Torah.

1902. M. Ostrow re-elected President. Synagogue enlarged to double its seating capacity.

1903. M. Ostrow re-elected President. Total of $1800.00 paid on purchase price of $4500.00. Deed to Synagogue property given to Congregation. Congregation gave mortgage for $2100.00. Mortgage on burying ground paid in full.

1904. I. Apple elected President. Congregation divided on account of Rabbi. About half of members left Congregation.

1905. D. Nemerovsky elected President. $500.00 paid on mortgage.

1906. D. Nemerovsky re-elected President. $500.00 paid on mortgage. Ladies Auxiliary Society organized. Mrs M. Barde President.

1907. D. Nemerovsky re-elected President. $600.00 paid on mortgage. Mrs M. Barde President Ladies Auxiliary Society.

1908. D. Nemerovsky re-elected President. Balance of mortgage $1100.00 paid in full. Ladies Auxiliary Society paying on note. Mrs I. Savransky President of Ladies Auxiliary Society.

1909. D. Nemerovsky re-elected President. Building Committee appointed. M. Ostrow chairman. $1006 amount of seat returns for Holidays turned over to Building Committee. Mrs I. Savransky President of Ladies Auxiliary Society.

1910. M. Gale elected President. $1203.00 amount of seat returns from Holidays turned over to Building Committee. M. Ostrow chairman. $7000 subscribed among officers and members towards the erection of a new Synagogue. Ladies Auxiliary Society paid up note of $200.00. Mrs M. Ostrow President of Ladies Auxiliary Society. Sabbath School Organized. M. Ostrow Supt.

1911. M. Gale re-elected President. May 1st contract signed for erection of new Synagogue to cost $24,000.00 not including furnishings. M. Ostrow chairman of Building Committee. Ladies Auxiliary Society donated Pews for new synagogue, to cost $1400.00. Mrs M. Ostrow President Ladies Auxiliary. Golden Rule Society organized among the Sabbath School children, by M. Ostrow Superintendent of Sabbath School. Miss Sadie Goldblatt President. Corner stone is being laid this day June 18th 1911.

Total membership of Congregation 121
" " Ladies Auxiliary 106
Pupils enrolled in Sabbath school 144

Information given by D. Nemerovsky.

Written by M. L. Gale.

Document from Neveh Zedek cornerstone, 1911. Courtesy, NS.

windows and we could hear him practice davening. It was a pleasure." When Rosencrantz died in 1936 at the age of 61, six months after a 20-year celebration in his honor, the *Scribe* noted that the funeral of this "beloved religious leader" as attended by "hundreds of sorrowing friends."

But the people who laid the cornerstone for Neveh Zedek's synagogue in 1911 had no way of knowing that the stone walls would resound for years to come with the beautiful voice of Abraham Rosencrantz. Ironically, Rosencrantz may well have attended the dedication ceremony as a representative of Shaarie Torah, since the rabbis of all Portland's congregations were there. Despite the differences between synagogues and services, this coming together to share one another's moments of joy is itself testimony to the fact that Portland's congregations—"Orthodox" and Reform alike— were not just growing, they were growing up.

The Secular "Synagogues": A Model of Lay Leadership

The decade immediately following the building of Ahavai Sholom's new synagogue witnessed the most substantial growth yet in the brief history of Portland, which emerged as one of the nation's leading exporters of lumber and wheat. In addition, the arrival of the automobile drastically changed the very concept of "city," along with the social life of Portlanders. But to Portland's Jewish population, perhaps the most significant development was the blooming of numerous organizations that would eventually replace the synagogues as the centers of Jewish social life.

Chief among these were various B'nai B'rith lodges, in which members of Ahavai Sholom would play a significant part. Of the principals recently cited, for example, both Morris Gilbert and Isaac Swett were heavily involved in the founding and growth of Lodge 314. Also, over half of the 15 original board members of the B'nai B'rith Building Association, formed in 1910, were members of Ahavai Sholom, including former or future congregational presidents Joseph Shemanski (1904-1906), Alex Miller (1918-1921 and 1924-1925), and John Dellar (1925-1927). In contrast to the wealthy Jews of German descent and the less well-to-do immigrants of South Portland, most of these members of Ahavai Sholom belonged to a new middle class, the emergence of which William Toll has called, "For Portland Jewry, the most important social event of the years just before and after World War I."

1892–1922 / Respecting the Past

If we were to single out one member of Ahavai Sholom to stand as a symbol of the changing Jewish social life in the first two decades of the twentieth century, that person would have to be David Solis-Cohen. Unlike all of the congregation leaders we have seen so far, Cohen was a native of the United States. He was born in 1850 into a prominent Sephardic family of Philadelphia. Though law would be his chosen career, his earliest ambitions seem to have been literary. Besides writing several plays and at least one book, he authored a number of newspaper columns in Philadelphia under the unlikely pseudonym of "Daisy Shortcut." In 1877 he moved to Oakland, California, where he became active as a fund-raiser, lay preacher, and a pioneer in the Young Men's Hebrew Association movement in the West. Though he remained in Oakland for only a year, his oratorical powers clearly inspired the Jewish community, including a local poetaster who wrote the following in the *Jewish Tribune:*

B'nai B'rith officers, 1921, including several Ahavai Sholom members. Seated, from left: Jess Rich, Alex Miller, Isaac Swett, Zeke Swett, Jonah Wise, David Solis-Cohen, Sam Mendelsohn, Alex Weinstein, Sigmund Lipman. Standing, from left: Sam Kohs, Milton Margulis, Jacob Lauterstein, Nathan Weinstein, Joseph Shemanski, Ben Rubin, Anselm Boskowitz, Sol Bishoff, Sam Tonkin, Edward Weinbaum. Courtesy, JHSO.

> Now, Oakland's representative, Cohen appears.
> And on his countenance a smile he wears;
> His words are manly, and his heart sincere;
> No wonder that his brethren him revere.
> Then up springs David with his martial air,
> Foams at the mouth, there's danger in his glare.
> O, do not give a permanent vacation
> To Cohen of the Y.M.H. Association.

Cohen arrived in Portland in 1878, and quickly became a lay pillar of both Beth Israel and Ahavai Sholom, exemplifying a pattern of dual membership that would become not uncommon as the century wore on. When, in 1880, Cohen produced and acted in his musical "Esther" at the Metropolitan Theatre, he donated the not inconsiderable profits of $2,500 in equal shares to congregations Beth Israel and Ahavai Sholom. This incident typifies Cohen's remarkable talents, energy and generosity, as well as his determination to bridge the ethnic and ritualistic barriers that persisted among the Jews of Portland.

In addition to his work for the synagogue and for B'nai B'rith Lodges 65 and 314, Cohen was a Royal Arch Mason, an Exalted Ruler of the Elks, and a Grand Master of the Ancient Order of United Workmen. One would be hard put, in fact, to find an organization of which Cohen was not a prominent member. What he didn't join, he was elected to, serving on the Oregon Board of Immigration for four years, as Commissioner of Charities and Corrections for six, and as Police Commissioner of Portland in 1890. In 1891 he was offered the Republican nomination for mayor of Portland, but declined—a rarity in his long public career.

But in Portland, as in Oakland, it was Cohen's power as a public speaker that brought him the most notice. No public event, whether religious or secular, could be considered major if Cohen was not invited to speak. (One commentator notes Cohen's distinction of having officiated at the laying of the cornerstones of every synagogue built during his 50 years in Portland and of several outside of Portland!) His most consistent theme—whether to an audience of Jews, Masons, Elks, or fellow Republicans—was how religious ritual supports American ethical traditions, reinforces habits of liberal fellowship, and thereby contributes to a humane and stable social order. While for non-Jewish audiences he often drew attention to the variety of rituals and denominations within Judaism as evi-

1892–1922 / Respecting the Past

David Solis-Cohen. During Cohen's 50 years in Portland, no civic or religious event was off-limits for his extraordianary talents as a speaker. Courtesy, JHSO.

dence of its vitality, to Jewish audiences he stressed the unity behind the diversity. As one commentator, Rabbi Julius Nodel, puts it, "In the development of Western Jewry, he was important in that he was one of the men who opposed drawing rigid lines of theological or ethnic differences. For him, Judaism was one whole concept. He threw his weight behind any movement that drew Jews from different factions closer together."

It was in this spirit that Cohen, along with Rabbi Jonah Wise and fellow lawyer Isaac Swett, filed the articles of incorporation for the B'nai B'rith Building Association in July of 1910. Besides hoping to promote a feeling of fellowship among the community's Jews, the founders of the Building Association envisioned a physical setting that would become the hub of cultural, recreational, and political activities. It was hardly coincidental that Cohen and many of the association's members were also among the prime advocates of Zionism in Portland. When war broke out in Europe, the urge to provide relief for Jewish refugees combined with the desire to unify the philanthropic activities of the community, a combination that provided fertile ground for the Zionist movement.

The B'nai B'rith Building, completed in 1914.

The B'nai B'rith Building, erected in 1914 on S.W. 13th Avenue between Mill and Market Streets, was a major step toward meeting these goals and toward the ultimate unification of all the B'nai B'rith Lodges in 1919. Cohen was elected president of the District Grand Lodge in 1921 and during his presidential tour to California and Nevada hammered home one of his favorite themes, the role of B'nai B'rith as an institution "essentially Jewish as it is American, seeking to promulgate the principles expressed both in the Bible and in the American Constitution."

Cohen was not only the most prominent promoter of Judaism within the community, but one of its chief defenders as well, especially against the brushfires of anti-Semitism that flared up in

Portland after World War I and that would put the torch to Ahavai Sholom's synagogue in 1923. Not only Cohen, but his sister, Salome Bernstein, and sister-in-law, Mrs. Isaac Lesser Cohen—both leaders of the Council of Jewish Women—were key figures in the formation of an anti-defamation committee in 1916. The committee investigated anti-Semitic slurs in local newspapers and on the vaudeville stage. Though none of Cohen's speeches on behalf of the committee survives, a passage that he delivered 25 years earlier on behalf of the oppressed Jews of Russia illustrates both the fervor of his feelings on the subject of anti-Semitism and the classic eloquence of his oratory:

> If my people were void of intellect, emotionless, with no aspirations but to live as does the beast until nature claims its carcass; if we were, as some see fit to pity us, a people too sordid for any thoughts save those of temporal gain; if we loved money so much more than do those of other faiths around us; if we employed more questionable means of obtaining it, or made a more usurous use of it when obtained; if we, indeed, felt ourselves to be abandoned of God, vile in the past, selfish in the present, and hopeless in the future, I should certainly not be here opening my heart before you. But it is unnecessary to submit to intelligent minds that such is not the case. Our history is an open book to all who care to read its pages.... Interwoven as it is with the annals of the world, it permeates every nerve and fiber of that world's being, and acting under a law superior to those of earthly conception or execution, it will continue an important factor in the spiritual progress of the world until the purpose of nature shall be accomplished.

David Solis-Cohen's final public address was given at the Succoth festival of Congregation Ahavai Sholom in 1928, the year of his death at the age of 78. A joint memorial service of Beth Israel, Ahavai Sholom, and Neveh Zedek marked his passing, and accolades poured in from the entire Portland community and beyond. But perhaps the most fitting tribute to this model of lay leadership was uttered two years earlier by another member of Ahavai Sholom, Isaac Swett, at a ceremony in Cohen's honor. "I have known [David Solis-Cohen] for 44 years," Swett observed, "and I have never known him to refuse any call made upon him by the Jews of this city."

The End of An Era

Besides bringing the seeds of anti-Semitism to Portland, the years following World War I also brought a major recession and general hard times for all of the city's synagogues. For Ahavai Sholom, this meant setting aside its plans to finally secure a rabbi who would attract new members and consolidate its role as the middle-ground alternative to Orthodox and Reform Judaism in Portland.

Immediately following the construction of their new synagogue, the congregation had raised great hopes by hiring Rabbi Wolff Willmer of Meridian, Mississippi. Willmer, a Polish Prussian with degrees from both Yale and Johns Hopkins Universities, had indeed revitalized the congregation, starting a literary club and a Jewish history circle. But he had stayed only a little more than a year, departing in 1907 to accept a pulpit in Houston, Texas. Since that time, the religious leadership had once again reverted to the faithful Robert Abrahamson, who, however revered he might be among the membership, was not likely to inspire growth or attract new blood. The congregation had periodically taken steps to remedy this situation, as when Abe Rosenstein and Nathan Weinstein, visiting New York on business in 1909, had consulted Solomon Schechter at the Jewish Theological Seminary about securing a rabbi from the East. But now, with the Ladies Auxiliary's fund-raising being the main source of money for interest on the mortgage and the upkeep of the synagogue, even hiring guest lecturers and Sunday School teachers became a financial burden.

By 1917, however, conditions had improved enough for the congregation to consider some creative financing as a solution to its need for a rabbi. The need itself was succinctly described by the congregation's secretary, Julius Cohn, in a letter to a New York rabbi who had inquired about the pulpit in Portland. Cohn described the congregation as made up of 85 members, most of them having been on the roll for years, with new recruits being mostly the sons of old-time members. His picture of Abrahamson was that of a "quite old" but "dearly beloved" man who did not lecture and who, in the opinion of many, did not provide the Sunday School with "proper instruction." What was needed, Cohn concluded, was "an up-to-date rabbi, teacher and preacher, one who is sufficiently Americanized and learned, and one who can easily and favorably mix with the Jewish population of Portland." He mentions in closing that Rabbi Jonah Wise of Beth Israel was of the opinion that Ahavai Sholom should be the largest congregation in Portland.

While nothing came of this exchange of letters, Cohn's opinion was apparently supported by the congregation as a whole. At the 1917 annual meeting the membership voted to pay for a new rabbi by taking out another mortgage on the building and by raising funds through subscriptions—both of these measures being universally preferred to the option of raising current members' dues.

The first rabbi to answer the congregation's call for an up-to-date rabbi was Arthur Montaz. We have no record of where he came from, but he didn't stay long. Hired for the High Holiday services of 1918 and subsequently elected for a two-year term, he seems to have stirred up considerable discord by May of 1919. When he asked to have his salary raised from $200 to $250 a month, he was refused on the grounds that membership wasn't large enough to afford the additional expense. By December the congregational minutes were noting that the membership was, in fact, dropping off because of Montaz' unpopularity—hardly what the congregation had hoped for or could afford. At this point the minutes lapse into the diplomacy not untypical of documents intended for the eyes of future generations. Apparently, Rabbi Montaz asked for and received two months' leave with pay to go to Chicago to take care of urgent family business. While there, the trustees suggested, he should perhaps look around for a congregation that could pay him the $250 a month, though he was "welcome" to return to Portland if he failed in that mission. When Montaz wrote back from Chicago asking if the congregation really wanted him back, however, he was told that "The Trustees and officers would be acting hypocritically" if they urged or invited him to return to the congregation. To his credit, Rabbi Montaz replied with a polite and cordial letter of resignation.

While Ahavai Sholom's search for a rabbi started anew, events of national scope left their mark on the congregation in varying degrees. The first was the devastating influenza epidemic of 1918-1919. We have no record of how many fatalities the congregation suffered, but the minutes show that many meetings were canceled and that religious school attendance dropped off sharply. On another front, 1919 also witnessed the passing of the 18th Amendment to the Constitution and the beginning of the Prohibition Era. While the amendment made provision for Jewish congregations to purchase wine to be used for Passover and other sacramental purposes, abuses of this provision were not uncommon nationwide. By way of preserving the spirit of the law, the trustees of Ahavai Sholom saw fit to stipulate that no new members would be accepted if it even appeared that they were joining to take advantage of wine privileges.

But recruiting new members was still a major concern, and, in lieu of an up-to-date rabbi, the congregation made several attempts to modernize. English prayer books were secured for the religious school; the practice of purchasing "honors" at the pulpit was abolished; the lighting in the choir was converted from gas to electricity because the gas fumes were "annoying and harmful." Bolstered by these improvements, the congregation returned to the matter at hand, convinced that they could do better than they had during Rabbi Montaz' short stay. Ironically, however, the next rabbi who was offered and accepted the position never even made it to Portland, except to be interviewed.

This was Rabbi Philip Kleinman, remembered by many current members as the rabbi of Neveh Zedek from 1937 to 1956. Rabbi Kleinman seems to have favorably impressed the members of Ahavai Sholom when he came from St. Paul, Minnesota, to be interviewed in August of 1921, for the minutes note that he was offered the pulpit and gladly accepted. But that is the last we hear of the matter. Were it not for the testimony of Mathew Kleinman, Rabbi Kleinman's son and a long-time member of Neveh Shalom, we would have no way of knowing what happened. "It's true." the younger Kleinman confirms:

> My father was offered a contract to be the rabbi of Congregation Ahavai Sholom in August of 1921, which he accepted. He arrived back home in St. Paul after a two-day train trip to tell my mother the good news. My mother had a four-day-long weekend to think things over with three small children, the youngest a four-month-old-baby! She simply told Dad that he would have to telephone the congregation in Portland that he had changed his mind and could not accept the position, since she absolutely refused to raise her boys in such a small Jewish community in Indian country! He could not change her mind, and regretfully had to notify the committee that he would not be able to come.

Apparently, Rabbi Kleinman did finally persuade his wife that the Indians in Portland weren't hostile, but only after sixteen years, when he accepted the pulpit at Congregation Neveh Zedek. (Mathew Kleinman notes that it was only then that his mother would open a box of embroidered handkerchiefs that his father had purchased for her at Meier and Frank's 16 years earlier!)

Hence, the 1921 High Holidays, which should have been conducted by Rabbi Kleinman, were in fact conducted by Rabbi Nahum Krueger, a graduate of the University of Pennsylvania and the Jewish Technological Seminary. Though Krueger's previous experience had been mostly at Jewish orphan homes and Hebrew schools, Ahavai Sholom would retain him as rabbi for the next four years—no small feat for a congregation that would see five rabbis come and go in the ten-year period between 1918 and 1928.

Rabbi Krueger's main contribution to the congregation, perhaps, was his role in formalizing its move from "orthodox" to Conservative Judaism by urging that it affiliate with the Conservative national organization, the United Synagogue of America, which had been formed in 1913. Ahavai Sholom formally joined in 1921 and was represented at the 1922 national convention in New York by Nathan and Moe Weinstein, who, along with Isaac Swett, Ben Pallay, Leon Semler, and the Holzman brothers, had been congregational leaders in the shift to formal Conservatism. In subsequent years, the synagogue would occasionally let its membership in the national organization lapse, but would always resume the affiliation.

Though strictly a formality, Ahavai Sholom's public acknowledgement of its adherence to Conservative Judaism does, in retrospect, stand as the end of an old order and the beginning of a new. The sense of this is heightened by the fact that, in July of 1922, death finally brought an end to Ahavai Sholom's long association with Rev. Robert Abrahamson, who had served the congregation for 37 of the previous 40 years. During those years, Abrahamson had accepted with grace whatever role was assigned him, humbly stepping aside whenever the congregation actively sought a full-time ordained rabbi. It was in the congregation that he had married and had seen his children grow up, and it was with the congregation that he and his wife, Anna, shared their grief when their young son died in 1913. In August of 1921 he had formally retired with the title of Rabbi Emeritus. In less than a year, he was dead.

Rabbi Philip Kleinman. Though he turned down the job at Ahavai Sholom in 1921, Kleinman became rabbi of Neveh Zedek in 1937 and went on to become a mainstay of the Jewish community in Portland. Courtesy, NS.

Rev. Robert Abrahamson and his wife, Anna. Courtesy, NS.

A fitting memorial to the compassion of Robert Abrahamson is the story of "Chief White Cloud." To fully appreciate the somewhat circuitous story, you have to start at the end.

A 16-year-old boy named Max Friedman was working in Nome, Alaska, during his first time away from his family.

Anxious to get home to Seattle for Rosh Hashanah, Friedman came to the docks several days before the boat was scheduled to arrive, and spent his time day-dreaming about home. One day he thought he heard a beautiful voice singing Kol Nidre. At first he thought that, in his eagerness to get home for the holidays, he was fantasizing, but the melody persisted. He walked around trying to find the source of the singing and finally located an Indian stevedore at one end of the dock. Friedman approached the stevedore and asked him if he knew what he was singing and where he had learned it.

It turned out that the stevedore had been born in Alaska and had exhibited unusual singing talent as a child. Since there were no schools in Alaska to train him, he was sent to the Chemawa Indian School in Oregon. There his voice developed. One day, an agent for the Pantages vaudeville circuit heard him and, after graduation, signed him up to perform on the circuit. The young singer was given a resplendent Indian costume and was billed as "Chief White Cloud." He traveled all over the country and was highly successful. Eventually, however, he developed a drinking problem and became more and more unreliable until, one day when he was in Portland, he was fired for good.

Penniless and dejected, the Indian was sitting on a curb in Portland bemoaning his lot when Rev. Abrahamson happened along. Abrahamson tapped him on the shoulder and asked him what his problems were. When the Indian had finished his tale of woe, Rev. Abrahamson took pity on him and invited him back to Ahavai Sholom, where he offered him a job in the synagogue choir. Taking the destitute but talented young man under his wing, Abrahamson taught him all the melodies for the Sabbath and holidays, including the Kol Nidre. The Indian sang for several years in the choir until his drinking problem resurfaced and he was caught selling umbrellas that he had stolen from the synagogue lobby to buy liquor. With great regret, Abrahamson had to dismiss him from the choir. Eventually, "Chief White Cloud" made his way to Alaska, where he found a job working—and singing—on the docks in Nome.

Rev. Abrahamson's death was noted throughout the entire Portland community and featured in all the local papers. A front-page article in the *Oregon Journal*, under the headline "Portland Rabbi Called by Death," is representative. "In the *Journal* office," the article reports, " as in hundreds of homes and stores and businesses, the news of the death of Rabbi Abrahamson was received as a shock. Each week it was his wont to come to the *Journal* editorial rooms with the notice he had prepared of his synagogue service, and the coming of this simple, kindly man was one of the bright events of the week."

Indeed, the coming—and staying—of this simple, kindly man was one of the bright events of the first 50 years of congregation Ahavai Sholom, and his going was the end of an era in its history.

1923-1939
The Disallowed Luxury

*Pessimism is a luxury
that a Jew can never allow himself.*
—Golda Meir

Snowmelt, tides, erosion. The forces that change the character of a river are often remote and imperceptible. Similarly, the causes of major changes in Portland's Jewish community during the twenties and thirties originated far from the Northwest, though their effects on the congregations were tangible enough.

World War I and the national xenophobia that followed radically changed the flow of Jewish immigration to the United States. As early as 1912, H. H. Goddard had been invited by the U.S. Public Health Service to screen arriving immigrants on Ellis Island with an eye to weeding out the "feebleminded." Applying the Binet tests of intelligence, Goddard concluded that 83 percent of the Jews, 87 percent of the Russians, 80 percent of the Hungarians, and 79 percent of the Italians tested were feebleminded. Partly as a result of Goddard's "scientific" research, deportations for mental deficiency increased to 350 percent in 1913 and 570 percent in 1914 over the average for the five preceding years.

The ultimate outcome of this trend was the passing, in 1924, of the Immigration Restriction Act. Significantly, quotas set by the act were calculated at two percent of people from each nation represented in the U.S. at the census of 1890, rather than on the more recent census of 1920. Since, as we've seen, the great influx of Eastern

The Aftermath of War: Cause for Fear

European Jews did not reach full force until after 1890, the quota for Jews effectively reduced the flow of Jewish immigrants to a trickle. In Portland, as elsewhere, the size of the Jewish population became more or less fixed at what it had been prior to the twenties.

Laws such as the Immigration Restriction Act do not sprout untended, but are bred from the soil of the country's mood. In this case, the mood of the country could prove decidedly ugly. Evidence of this in the Northwest was the rise to prominence of the Ku Klux Klan in the 1920s. While directing the bulk of their hate against Catholics, the Klan was openly anti-Semetic as well, and may have been responsible for the fires that destroyed two of Portland's synagogues.

At 6:30 on the evening of November 5, 1923, a 16-year-old boy named Abie Singer noticed smoke pouring from the roof of Ahavai Sholom synagogue. Alert, he broke the nearby fire-alarm box and summoned the fire department. By the time firemen arrived, the roof was ablaze and the fire, which had started in the main floor and shot to the upper stories through an air vent, was showering sparks and pieces of cornice on the crowd below. A member of the congregation, William Schlosberg, dashed into the building at the risk of his life and removed two of the scrolls from the sanctuary. He was followed by the president of the congregation, Sam Swirsky, who rescued various sacramental vessels, and by Rabbi Krueger, who vainly attempted to protect his 1,000-volume library of rare books, most of which were badly damaged by water. When the blaze was finally under control, firemen discovered a number of rags under the pulpit, where the fire had started. No perpetrator was ever apprehended, but the fire was assumed to have been started by an arsonist. This assumption was strengthened when, less that a month later, Beth Israel's synagogue at S.W. 12th and Main Street was the target of an arsonist's attack.

Ku Klux Klan in Portland, 1923. Courtesy, OHS.

70

As William Toll points out, the decision as to what to do about reconstructing their respective synagogues highlights a major difference between the two congregations. After considerable debate between the younger and older factions within the congregation, Beth Israel decided to build a much larger structure at a new site, one less dominated by apartment houses and grocery stores. They purchased a square block between N.W. Glisan and Flanders Streets for $65,000 and proceeded to raise and borrow $300,000 to construct a beautiful domed temple.

By contrast, Ahavai Sholom used its insurance payment and a $10,000 loan to repair the old building. This decision was strongly opposed by Rabbi Krueger and by an editorial in the *Scribe* of November 30, 1923. The editorial notes three options: "to build on the old site, to fuse with the Noveh [sic] Zedek Talmud Torah Congregation and to rebuild on the East Side." Of the three, rebuilding on the old site was the "least desirable." The author of the editorial argues that "The Jews of Portland have already sufficient centrally located synagogues to meet their needs," that Ahavai Sholom "has made but little progress" being "hemmed in between the reform and orthodox congregations," and that rebuilding on the same site would mean that congregation could not "hope to be a greater factor in the immediate future than it has been in the past." After dismissing the merger plan as being "an argument from a sense of weakness," the editorial recommends rebuilding on the East Side as the "ideal" solution. (The proposition was one that would resurface in 1934 and again in 1961 when Ahavai Sholom and Neveh Zedek did merge.) The *Scribe* editorial continues:

> The population of Portland is growing. The number of Jews living on the East Side is large and rather centrally located. If the Ahavai Sholom Congregation were to sell its present property, rebuild in the Irvington district and conduct a neighborhood synagogue it could and would meet a need which is apparent and which will some day have to be met in another way. There is a large field in the district indicated, and rather than continue in a slowly growing manner or give up its identity the congregation ought to be willing to take the risk of building where it is at present needed.

Whatever the merits of this argument, the membership of Ahavai Sholom was not in the mood for risk-taking. Consequently, the congregation proceeded to raise the necessary funds while bemoaning the decline in membership. In the meantime, when both the proposed merger and the plans for a new structure were rejected, Rabbi Krueger decided to return to his former post in New York, leaving the congregation with its perennial problem of finding a new spiritual leader.

Despite these setbacks, the rebuilt synagogue included some significant improvements, so much so that the Oregon Journal described it as having "the appearance of a new structure." Its "fine interior" boasted an enlarged auditorium and schoolroom, a Wurlitzer pipe organ in place of the small reed organ, and an electrical Ner Tamid to replace the old gas Eternal Light. On June 5, 1924, the "new" synagogue was rededicated with a ceremony that included Rabbi Jonah Wise of Temple Beth Israel, Rabbi Samuel Sachs of Congregation Neveh Zedek, Rabbi J. B. Fain of Congregation Shaarie Torah, and, of course, a dedicatory speech by David Solis-Cohen. The new Eternal Light was switched on and the congregation symbolically entered the modern age, little knowing what trials lay ahead.

Rabbi Nahum Krueger and the 1924 Ahavai Sholom confirmation class. Shortly after this photo was taken, Rabbi Krueger resigned and returned to New York. Courtesy, JHSO.

Program for the rededication of Congregation Ahavai Sholom after the synagogue was damaged by fire in 1923. Courtesy, NS.

Following A River

The Aftermath of War: Cause for Hope

If the years following World War I brought a tide of xenophobia, however, they also brought a wave of new hope that would also reach the banks of Portland's Jewish community, this time from as far away as England.

"I have much pleasure in conveying to you, on behalf of His Majesty's Government, the following declaration of sympathy with Jewish Zionist aspirations which has been submitted to and approved by the Cabinet." Thus began the famous letter of November 2, 1917, from the British Foreign Secretary, Arthur James Balfour, to Lord Walter Rothschild, a document later to be known as the Balfour Declaration. Written in acknowledgement of the distinguished war record of the Jewish Legion, the Balfour Declaration sent a wave of rejoicing through the Jewish world. The long-awaited establishment of the Jewish State seemed at hand. In Portland, as elsewhere, the pulse of those who had worked long and hard in support of the Zionist movement beat faster.

As Deborah Goldberg points out in her thesis on "Jewish Spirit on the Urban Frontier," Zionism in Portland reflected two distinct and somewhat paradoxical characteristics of the city itself. On the one hand, it appealed to the agricultural and pioneer spirit that had moved many of Portland's original Jews to come to the Northwest. The appeal of this "return to the soil" movement went beyond the farming class to include professionals, such as Isaac Swett, whose family roots were agricultural, and others, such as Stephen Wise, who had never lived on a farm but who saw the movement as physically and morally beneficial to Jewish youth.

The other appeal of Zionism lay in its philanthropic, cultural side. The very remoteness of Portland created a general anxiety about losing touch with Jewish activities and causes around the world. Zionism provided both a cultural bridge to the world community of Jews and a concrete means of performing good deeds. It was this latter, philanthropic aspect of Zionism that appealed to the ever-practical Portlanders, who had far less inclination to debate the ideological implications of Zionism than did their counterparts in Europe or the eastern United States.

No single organization is more representative of the Zionist emphasis on practical, charitable deeds than Hadassah, the Women's Zionist Organization of America. The Portland chapter was founded in the early twenties by Paula Heller Lauterstein, whose father, Henry Nathan Heller, was the rabbi of Neveh Zedek for several years. Born in Copenhagen, Paula Heller had married a clothes merchant named Jacob Lauterstein, who—like Joseph Nudelman, Solomon Dellar (whose son John was later a president of Ahavai Shalom), and several other early members of Neveh Zedek—had emigrated to Portland after unsuccessful attempts at farming in North Dakota.

Nationally, Hadassah supported any number of programs associated with Palestine, including an extensive health care program and regular contributions to the Jewish National Fund (JNF). In Portland, as elsewhere, funds were raised mainly by the sale of

The Heller family in Copenhagen in 1896 before emigrating to Portland. Paula Heller Lauterstein, seated directly in front of her mother, founded Hadassah in Portland. Her father, Henry Nathan Heller (standing), was rabbi of Neveh Zedek from 1907 to 1911. Courtesy, Felice Lauterstein Driesen.

homemade plum puddings during the winter holidays and by contributions to the Hadassah-sponsored JNF "Blue Box," which would be a familiar sight in Jewish homes and schools well into the thirties and forties. Current Neveh Shalom member Toinette Menashe recalls the "field trips to the Newsreel Theatre on Washington Street in the late thirties to see grainy documentary films on Jewish pioneer life in the Yishuv"—adding, "we could hardly wait to fill our blue boxes to provide monies for all those plantings!" In Portland, Hadassah also generated numerous smaller auxiliaries, including sewing circles and study groups.

Congregations Neveh Zedek and Ahavai Sholom were the

Stephen Wise, Beth Israel's dynamic young rabbi, in 1906. Wise was a regular guest speaker at Congregation Ahavai Sholom. Courtesy, Temple Beth Israel.

community leaders in Zionist activities of this kind, even to the point of mild rivalry. As the Zionist movement grew, Neveh Zedek founded the Kadima Society, a group of high school students interested in Zionism, and Ahavai Sholom invited Golda Myerson—later Golda Meir, Prime Minister of Israel—to speak to the congregation about the Histadruth labor movement in Palestine.

In all of these Zionist activities, the overiding tone was secular, as opposed to explicitly religious, though many of Portland's rabbis were also extremely devoted to the Zionist cause. In this context, we think first of Beth Israel's Rabbi Stephen Wise, who was a close friend of the great Zionist figure, Theodor Herzl, and whose ardent devotion to the cause was unusual for a leader of a Reform congregation. But while none of the rabbis of Ahavai Sholom or Neveh Zedek rivaled Wise as a national figure, many of them shared his zeal for the Zionist movement. For example, Rabbi Philip Kleinman of Neveh Zedek consistently underscored the religious implications of Zionism, going so far as to declare that "For me, Zionism is Judaism." Kleinman explained in an interview in 1981: "We didn't create anything new. The thousands of years that we have been away from Zion after the destruction of the first and second Temples have not taken Zion out of us. It has been within us, and whether it is on the Sabbath, or on the festivals, daily when we pray, we say 'Oh God, may our eyes turn to Zion.' "

As for the rabbis of Ahavai Sholom, it might justly be said that, given the rapidity of their turnover between 1924 and 1933, their commitment to the Zionist cause supplied one of the few elements of continuity. With the exception of Herbert Parzen, none of Ahavai Sholom's rabbis during this difficult period lasted more than a year. Consequently, the congregation was forced to resort to its own spiritual resources in this as in other matters. The prevailing senti-

1923–1939 / The Disallowed Luxury

ment of the congregation was voiced by Sam Swirsky in his president's report of 1927: "Rabbis come and go but this House of Worship is going to be forever. We must continue to go forward."

"Rabbis Come and Go"

"We were very fortunate to have had the opportunity to release Rabbi Teshnor from his contract, for had he remained, our financial condition would have been greatly impaired." This candid observation of Alex Miller's, in his president's report to Ahavai Sholom in 1925, underscores the dilemma that plagued the congregation throughout the twenties. In contrast to earlier years, when the issue of short-term rabbis seemed to hinge on questions of character, the pre-depression years found Ahavai Sholom unable to support a rabbi and still stay afloat financially. Miller and others, however, were also keenly aware that a synagogue without a rabbi was "like ship at sea without a master." Ironically, it was the very persistence of their financial problems that prepared Ahavai Sholom to weather the depression with much less difficulty than the wealthier Beth Israel. As William Toll notes, Temple Beth Israel seemed to be in a continual state of financial crisis during the Depression, whereas Ahavai Sholom, "with low dues, salaries, and budgets, and with very limited communal ambitions and contacts...seemed most concerned with raising small amounts of money to meet current demands." And while Ahavai Sholom's membership had fallen from 277 in 1923 (just prior to the fire) to 169 in 1928, it declined only slightly further during the Depression, reaching a low of 152 in 1934.

The Rabbi Teshnor to whom Alex Miller was referring in his president's report was Maurice Teshnor, who had been hired when Rabbi Krueger returned to New York in 1924. Also from the East, Teshnor had held pulpits in Long Island and Jersey City, where both he and his wife had been active in Zionist circles. The congregation was apparently satisfied with Teshnor, for they offered him another year's contract in April of 1925. But before the next High Holidays, Rabbi Teshnor was gone, prompting Alex Miller's baleful assessment of the congregation's finances. Ahavai Sholom would have to get through the High Holidays as best it could under the circumstances.

In the meantime, the congregation came into some much-needed good fortune in the form of a bequest from a member named A. Wildman. Wildman had decided to deed to the congregation the sum of $20,000 upon his death. But on August 19, 1925, the board moved that "the giver should be visited to induce him to give the sum now, while he can enjoy the results of his generosity." Apparently, Wildman was persuaded by this disinterested appeal to his best interests, for by May of 1926 the congregation was using the Wildman fund to hire a new rabbi.

This was Elliott Burstein, a graduate of Columbia University and of the Jewish Theological Seminary, who brought with him three years' experience at a Conservative congregation in Salt Lake City. Strikingly handsome at 27, Burstein was one of the youngest rabbis in the country, a fact that raised a few eyebrows among members of the Ladies Auxiliary, which went on record as preferring an older man. Burstein's obvious qualifications won out, however, and he was hired.

We have no record of why Rabbi Burstein stayed with the congregation only a year and a half—through the High Holidays of 1927—but his short stay seems to have had some positive results. On Burstein's departure, President Sam Swirsky noted that membership had increased, services were better attended, and the school had grown rapidly. Apparently, Burstein's youthful vigor had given

Elliott Burstein (left), rabbi of Ahavai Sholom, 1926-1927, and Rabbi Herbert Parzen. Parzen's four-year stay at Ahavai Sholom (1928-1932) was longer than that of any ordained rabbi before him. Courtesy, OHS.

1923–1939 / The Disallowed Luxury

the congregation a much-needed shot in the arm— though whether the inoculation would take remained to be seen.

Ahavai Sholom's next rabbi, its fifth in 10 years, was Herbert Parzen, who was elected to the pulpit in January of 1928. Parzen came to Portland from Temple Aaron in St. Paul, Minnesota, having graduated from the University of Michigan and the Jewish Theological Seminary. He would remain with the synagogue for four years, a congregational record for an ordained rabbi up to that point. His tenure coincided both with a catastrophic period in American history—the Great Depression—and with an obscure period in congregational history. For reasons not clear, no board minutes have survived from November 1928 to January 1934, if indeed the minutes were ever kept. (It is interesting to note in passing that the congregational minutes stop in the same month that marked the death of David Solis-Cohen, as though out of respect for the silencing of that great voice.) What little we know of synagogue activities during this period is derived from various reports in the *Scribe*.

On the other hand, 1931 is one of the few years for which we have a surviving document from Congregation Neveh Zedek. As mentioned earlier, the minutes for that congregation have been lost—an especially regrettable circumstance in light of the fact that Neveh Zedek had the same recording secretary, Dr. George Rubenstein, from 1902 until at least 1927. Thanks, however, to a personal daily diary kept by President Jacob Asher for the year 1931, we are able to reconstruct something of the hard times of the Depression.

Many of Asher's entries have to do with internal conflict between himself and the rabbi, whose attendance at the daily minyan was not up to Asher's standards. (Asher himself rarely

Jacob Asher, president of Neveh Zedek from 1930 to 1931. Asher's daily diary during his presidency constitutes one of the few written records that we have from Neveh Zedek. Courtesy, the Asher family.

missed a minyan or a Sabbath service, rating attendance at the latter as "poor," "fair," "good," or "nice," and carefully noting whether or not the rabbi was present at minyan.) As might be expected, however, the congregation's dominating concern was finances. Asher's diary notes that in July of 1931, the congregation was $4,000 in debt. Two courses of action were proposed: take out a new mortgage on the synagogue (the old one had been paid off in 1920), or cut salaries. Neither alternative being particularly attractive, a decision was postponed until after the High Holidays. Then, on October 11, a "well-attended but disorderly" meeting was held, the outcome of which was a decision to cut salaries and make a concerted effort to collect delinquent dues. Not surprisingly, this was hardly a popular decision among those whose salaries were being cut, and the rabbi's attendance at the minyan seems to have declined even further. On October 22, Asher asked the board to give him power to force the rabbi to attend services, but it refused, perhaps feeling that sermons by a reluctant rabbi would be worse than no sermons at all. Fed up, Asher announced that he would not be a candidate for reelection, and stuck by this decision despite pleading from various quarters. In spite of this wrangling, however, Asher notes that the year ended on an upbeat note. The congregation celebrated the 20th anniversary of their building by dedicating a Sefer Torah in honor of Oregon's Jewish governor, Julius Meier, and by holding special services featuring rabbis and cantors from all of Portland's congregations.

The rabbi with whom Asher had so much trouble was Meyer Rubin. Comparing the lists of rabbis and presidents for Neveh Zedek, we note an interesting fact about Rabbi Rubin—that his tenure corresponds to five of the six years between 1905 and 1935 that neither David Nemerovsky nor Marcus Gale served as president. Gale stepped down as president in 1928, the year Rabbi Rubin arrived, and reassumed office in 1935, the year Rubin left. If we were to read between the lines here, we might conjecture that Rabbi Rubin antagonized not only Asher, but also those two pillars of Neveh Zedek, Nemerovsky and Gale. Or it may be that he felt that these two men had too strong a hold on the congregation.

Conjecture aside, we know almost nothing about Rubin, except that he graduated from Harvard and Columbia Universities and—like his predecessor, Rabbi Samuel Sachs—trained at the Jewish Theological Seminary. This in itself is noteworthy, since part of the problem of maintaining an ordained rabbi hinged on the relative scarcity of American trained rabbis during the first quarter of this

In contrast to the unstable spiritual leadership at Neveh Zedek until the arrival of Rabbi Philip Kleinman in 1937, the lay leadership from 1905 to 1935 was largely a two-man show commandeered by David Nemerovsky and Marcus Gale.

David Nemerovsky was born in Russia in 1870 and came to the United State in 1886. An obituary notice in the Oregonian for October 14, 1953, refers to him as a "founder" of Neveh Zedek. According to Rabbi Albert Ruskin's 1936 recollections on Neveh Zedek's history, it was during Nemerovsky's first presidency (1905) that "the balcony relinquished its sole claim to women worshippers, and men and women were seated together." This bold move elicited "vehement protests on the part of the over-conservative, which resulted in several resignations."

David Nemerovsky

Nemerovsky served as president of the congregation from 1905 to 1909, from 1913 to 1914, and again from 1917 to 1924, a total of 15 years. For more than 50 years, he was also president of the Jewish Relief Society, an office that he held at his death.

Polish-born Marcus Gale came to the United States as a boy and worked as a harvest hand before taking up a homestead in North Dakota. After ten years of farming, he moved to Portland, where he became engaged in the mercantile business. He served as president of Neveh Zedek from 1910 to 1912, from 1925 to 1928, and from 1933 to 1934.

Gale's first term of office coincided with the the building of Neveh Zedek's synagogue on Sixth and Hall. Of that time, Rabbi Ruskin recalled: "Two faithful watchmen were there: hardy and determined Mr. Gale, and gentle, soft-spoken Mr. M. Ostrow. Their own places of business knew them not until September 1911, when the new synagogue opened its doors for dedication."

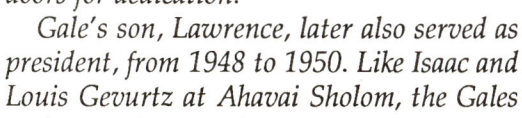

Marcus Gale

Gale's son, Lawrence, later also served as president, from 1948 to 1950. Like Isaac and Louis Gevurtz at Ahavai Sholom, the Gales were the only father and son to be presidents of their congregation.

Following A River

century. Rabbi Heller had been trained in Europe, and between his departure in 1911 and Sach's arrival in 1922 there is no rabbi of record at Neveh Zedek (in congregational notices, the newspapers usually listed Cantor Abraham Rosencrantz as "Rabbi"). The next 15 years saw four rabbis come and go: Sachs, Rubin, Abraham Israelitan, and Albert Ruskin. It was not until 1937, with the arrival of Philip Kleinman, that Neveh Zedek's spiritual leadership became stable.

Rabbis Meyer Rubin (left) and Samuel Sachs, Neveh Zedek's first two American-trained rabbis. Courtesy, OHS.

As for Rabbi Parzen at Ahavai Sholom, though we have no minutes to document his stay, we do know from other sources that he went on to be recognized as a leading Conservative rabbi and scholar, and that his association with Ahavai Sholom significantly contributed to its national stature. Besides writing a weekly column of commentary for the *Scribe*—a role previously reserved to Portland's nationally known Reform rabbis—Parzen wrote articles for the *Jewish Encyclopedia* and the *American Journal of Semitic Languages*. Like his immediate predecessors and successors, he was active in the Zionist cause, serving as president of the Portland Zionist Organization. At the synagogue, he revived the Men's Club and initiated the Rashi Club, a study group for young people. The Rashi Club met twice monthly to discuss such topics as intermarriage, the Balfour Declaration, the Zionist movement, and the works of Jewish authors, complementing their meetings with theatre parties and picnics. A recently departed member of Neveh Shalom, Nathan Berkham,

1923–1939 / The Disallowed Luxury

who was a student at Reed College at the time, was appointed advisor to the club on Parzen's departure. He recalled Rabbi Parzen as an intellectual who could seem somewhat distant, but with whom he personally maintained a warm relationship for the rest of Parzen's life. He also confirmed that the reason for Parzen's departure in 1932 was that the congregation said it could not afford his salary.

Ahavai Sholom's next rabbi, Raphael Goldenstein, was unique in two respects: he was the first "Portlander" to occupy a pulpit in his home town (he had been born in Russia but had grown up in

Rabbi Raphael Goldenstein with Ahavai Sholom confirmation class, 1933. Goldenstein's tenure at Ahavai Sholom was cut short by his untimely death in 1933. Courtesy, JHSO.

Portland), and he was the only rabbi at either Ahavai Sholom or Neveh Zedek to have been trained at the Hebrew Union College, the Reform Jewish seminary. As a youth, Goldenstein had taught at Temple Beth Israel under Rabbis Stephen Wise and Jonah Wise, and later distinguished himself as a translator of Russian works, including Leo Tolstoy's "What Is A Jew." His love for the city of Portland seemed to bode well for a long tenure at Ahavai Sholom, despite the congregation's financial hardships. Unfortunately, however, in July of 1933, barely a year and a half after he had arrived, Rabbi Goldenstein died suddenly of complications following a major operation. He was only 47 years old.

In contrast to Ahavai Sholom's almost chronic inability to retain a rabbi during this difficult period was its singular good fortune in acquiring the services of Sam Caplan and Cantor Morris Ail. Caplan, a former junk dealer, had come to Ahavai Sholom in 1918, and would serve the congregation as shammes until ill health forced him to retire in 1939. His duties included reading from the Torah, blowing the shofar, and collecting the dues. That Caplan was held in high regard despite this latter duty is itself testimony to the quality of his dedication to the synagogue for over 20 years.

Morris Ail, who arrived in 1925 and would remain with the synagogue for the next 36 years, marked a transition from the untrained, part-time cantor, such as his predecessor Hillel Slifman,

Cantor Morris Ail. Ail became an institution at Ahavai Sholom, serving it for over 35 years. Courtesy, NS.

and the full-time cantor, such as his successor Arthur Yolkoff, whom the congregation could afford to hire when it later merged with Neveh Zedek. Ail's family had originated in Odessa, Russia, and, when World War I blocked westward exit from Europe, had traveled across Siberia to China, then on to Japan, from whence they sailed to Seattle—an untypical route for most Jews, but one followed by other Portland Jewish families as well. Established in Portland, Ail made his living as the owner-manager of a print shop near S.W. Tenth and Washington and sang in the choir before becoming Ahavai Sholom's cantor and a familiar and beloved figure at religious school assemblies. Today, the Ail Music Room stands as a tribute to the memory of Morris Ail, a congregational treasure acquired in a period of financial hardship.

1923–1939 / The Disallowed Luxury

Despite shifts in leadership and the general hard times of the Depression, life at Ahavai Sholom went on. The *Scribe* contains reports of Sisterhood luncheons, Hanukkah parties, and Purim balls. It also notes some substantial improvements, such as the dedication of a chapel at Ahavai Sholom cemetery in 1930 and the purchase of a new oil furnace, made possible through a fund-raiser organized by the ever-active Sisterhood. William Toll, in *The Making of an Ethnic Middle Class*, provides an aerial view of the synagogue during this period:

Balancing the Spiritual and Financial Budgets

> At Ahavai Sholom the sisterhood held social events to raise funds for which a religious school building was contemplated. The process took the entire decade, with the mortgage being refinanced several times, yet never exceeding $5,000. The rabbi's salary fluctuated between $3,000 and $4,000 annually, while the salaries of the religious-school teachers were paid in part from tuition fees but largely from the interest on the bequest from the Wildman fund. While officers like Sam Swirsky, J. J. Shecter, and Mrs. Nathan Weinstein might take pride in their [congregation's] relative solvency, their major innovation during the decade was to introduce a form of junior membership for unmarried people under age 35 to accommodate the demographic changes which produced an enlarged clientele for the religious school.

As Toll's observation reminds us, two of Ahavai Sholom's most important resources in balancing the religious and financial budgets during these difficult years were the Sisterhood and the religious school. Educating the young in Jewish history and values had been central to the congregation's mission since the early days of Rabbi Eckman, and the very survival of the religious school became an issue during this period of unstable spiritual leadership and financial hardship. That the religious school not only survived but thrived during the thirties was due at least in part to the work and influence of a man known affectionately to a whole generation of Jewish children as "Uncle Louie": Louis Gevurtz.

Gevurtz served the congregation as president from 1928 to 1931 and again from 1940 to 1945. But it is for his leadership role in the religious school that he is remembered with most affection. His daughter, Suzanne Gevurtz Itkin, recalls:

> The synagogue religious school was his special project on whose behalf no amount of effort was too great. He was convinced that the

Louis Gevurtz, son of Isaac Gevurtz, in the 1930s. Known and loved by several generations of school children as "Uncle Louie," Gevurtz was president of Ahavai Sholom from 1928-1931, and again from 1940-1945. Courtesy, the Gevurtz family.

Two pillars of Ahavai Shalom: Cantor Morris Ail (left) and Louis Gevurtz. The occasion is a testimonial dinner in honor of Gevurtz on May 19, 1957. Courtesy, NS.

future of the Jewish people lay in the education of its youth in the history and customs, but more importantly, in the ethical teachings of Judaism. That the Sunday School kids might not forget him and what he stood for even for the two or three weeks a year he spent in California, boxes of oranges—at least one for each member present—arrived on a Sunday near Purim, and were as important a part of that celebration as were our costumes, noisemakers, and parade. He led us in marching around the sanctuary on Simchat Torah, following the Cantor and Rabbi, singing and waving our flags, but never lost in the celebration the opportunity to review for us the historical and philosophical importance of the Holiday.... Our car was always overflowing on the way to Sunday School with children whose parents, he thought, might not make the effort to get them there.

Gevurtz's participation in the life of the synagogue and of the community went far beyond his role in the religious school, but the contribution he made to his "special project" over the years was, by any standard, immeasurable.

A perpetual problem facing Gevurtz and others involved in the education of the young was lack of space. Toinette Menashe, whose student years began in 1936, recalls the "joyous holiday observances in the small basement vestry room." "Every inch of space was utilized," Menashe notes, "with classes held in front of the sanctuary, the back rows of the same sanctuary, and as young teenagers we graduated to 'the heights' and were assigned the balcony!"

Alleviating the physical and other problems encountered by the religious school was one of the many causes undertaken by the Sisterhood. Indeed, the earliest record of a woman's group in the congregation states: "The Ladies Aux [sic] Society of the Congregation Ahavai Sholom was instituted Sept 1899 with 44 members. Its aims and objects are to maintain the Sunday and Hebrew Schools of the Congregation." In hard times, "maintenance" usually translated to "fund-raising," and the Sisterhood could always be counted on to underwrite holiday celebrations, building campaigns, and substantial scholarship support.

In 1929, the Ahavai Sholom Sisterhood became affiliated with the Women's League for Conservative Judaism, the parent organization of women's groups from Conservative synagogues. Today, the Women's League, whose membership includes over 200,000 women, offers the Sisterhood programs on Jewish education, administrative training, and community involvement. In turn, Sister-

Following A River

Rabbi Edward Sandrow with his first confirmation class at Ahavai Sholom, 1934 (right, courtesy, Elaine Barde), and his last confirmation class, 1937 (below, courtesy, Delphine Davis and Irene Harrowitz). The size of the respective classes reflects the general growth in membership during Sandrow's tenure.

hood board members represent their organization at regional and national conventions of the Woman's League. During the Depression, however, the emphasis was on survival, and, as always, the Sisterhood came through.

Another Missed Merger

That Ahavai Sholom's decline in membership began to turn around in 1934 can be attributed in part to the arrival, for the 1933 High Holiday services, of Rabbi Edward T. Sandrow, who would remain for the next four years. Only 27 when he arrived in Portland, Sandrow went on to become an outstanding national and international figure in Conservative Judaism.

A list of Sandrow's achievements supplied by Temple Beth El in Cedarhurst, Long Island, where he went upon leaving Ahavai Sholom, runs to three typewritten pages and is far too long to include here. It notes, among other things, that he was the first rabbi to receive the National Community Service Award given by the Jewish Theological Seminary of America (where a chair in Pastoral Psychiatry is now named for him), that he was President of the Jewish Chaplain's Association of the U.S. Armed Forces and was a major at the time of his discharge, and that he accompanied Martin Luther King, Jr. on his march to Washington D.C. in 1963. Even more impressive as testimony to the force of his personality, perhaps, is the fact that he came to Temple Beth El when it was a congregation of 50 families and left it as a congregation of more than 900 families.

In 1933 these accomplishments lay ahead, but one can imagine how fortunate congregation Ahavai Sholom must have felt to have found such a man at such a time. Sandrow was not the first nor would he be the last, however, to learn that Portland, despite its reputation for inclement weather, was not a community that could be taken by storm. On the contrary, its response to originality and innovation has probably always struck outsiders, especially those from the East, as something less than enthusiastic. Thus, when one of Rabbi Sandrow's first acts was to propose a merger between Ahavai Sholom and Neveh Zedek, the results were somewhat predictable.

In defending his reasons for the proposed merger in the *Scribe* in 1934, Sandrow reveals the global sweep of his vision. "From the first moment in which I stepped into the community," he writes, from pulpit and from platform, have I preached, argued, and spoken for Jewish unity. In view of conditions confronting the Jews throughout the world [Hitler had come to power in Germany the year before], I felt as many of our leaders felt, that the time would have to come when Jewry throughout the world will have to be united actually as well as spiritually. I urged a central Jewish organization composed of all shades of opinion so that we may better be able to deal with our manifold communal problems.

Sandrow goes on to cite local conditions in support of his case: that Portland had never been large enough to house two Conservative congregations, that keeping up both synagogues wasted an emormous amount of financial energy, that the members of the two religious organizations shared a similar platform and attitude toward Jewish life, and that "merely an understanding and, if necessary, a little compromise could transform them into one large solid organization."

Despite the force of Sandrow's arguments, however, and the eagerness of Congregation Ahavai Sholom to seal the merger, the members of Neveh Zedek rejected the proposal. "As President of Congregation Neveh Zedek," Marcus Gale observed non-commitally, "I abide by the decision of our membership." The Jewish community, however, expressed great disappointment. "At a time when Jewish unity is so desperately needed," Samuel Weinstein commented, "members of these congregations had the opportunity to furnish a glorious example that would have brought untold benefits." David Robinson went further: "My inclination is to express irritation at the conduct of those strong personalities who are unwilling to subordinate self for the greater good of the group," he observed, adding somewhat prophetically: "I want to express the sincere hope for further deliberation between these two congregations. Surely where so many reasons can be advanced for unity there must be a way in which it can be reached." As for Rabbi Sandrow, his response betrays genuine bitterness. "Far be it from me," he begins, "to censure Neveh Zedek." But censure he does: "One cannot blame a congregation for the selfishness, short-sightedness and vanity of some of its members. Would that our prophets were alive today to cry out against the smugness, conceit, and stiff-neckedness of many of our people."

Clearly, Rabbi Edward Sandrow was a young man who wanted to get things done, and Portland, in the long haul, would not prove the most fertile ground for his zeal. Still, his contributions to Ahavai

Sholom and to the Jewish community were substantial, and came at a time when leadership was sorely needed. He launched successful drives to increase membership in both the synagogue and the religious schools. He organized the Young People's League. Elected to the National Education Committee of the Zionist Organization of America in 1934, he delivered numerous memorable sermons on Zionism and was personally responsible for Golda Meir's earlier-mentioned visit to Portland. Most importantly, perhaps more than anyone since Rabbi Eckman, he created a sense of possibilities for the congregation and set a standard of intellectual achievement and moral integrity for the rabbis who would follow him.

In the long run, then, through good fortune and bad, Congregation Ahavai Sholom weathered the Depression years as well as or better than most. Louis Gevurtz, in the annual report that marked the end of his first term as president (1928-1931), summed up the congregation's prevailing, if occasionally unwarranted, optimism: "While we are not in flourishing financial condition, we are perhaps not as involved as many other Jewish organizations and congregations here and elsewhere; and with the program the incoming officers will probably put into operation, there is no doubt in my mind that in that regard we have nothing to fear."

Elsewhere, however, the climate of the late thirties was palpable with reasons for fear. "In the darkening hours of 1938-39," Toinette Menashe recalls, "we [children in the religious school] were apprised by our teachers that Jewish refugee children would be joining our class, that they would be wearing clothing different from ours, and that we must be helpful, welcoming, and polite. How well I remember the mutual staring. It was through these children that we first became aware of the impending war in Europe, never dreaming of the devastating effects on our Jewish brethren there."

1940-1960
Journeys of Chance

"O river, O river, lend me a pitcher of water
for a journey that has chanced to me."
—The Talmud

[From the logbook of Sally Scheuer and the observations of his wife, Hedwig Scheuer, longtime current members of Neveh Shalom.]

Rumors and Roomers from Afar

May 18, 1936: *Leaving Fritzlar we took a local train to Kassel where we boarded a D-Zug (express train) to Hamburg. . . . We found a compartment and sat down. Pretty soon some people came with outstretched (uplifted) arms and greeted us with "Heil Hitler." When we answered with a polite "Guten Tag" they left and stood up in the narrow, crowded passageway rather than share the compartment with us. That happened five or six times and we were left with the compartment, that would hold 8 people, all to ourselves [Sally, Hedwig, and their six-year-old son, Ernest] This incident, among others, contributed to making it easier for us to leave Germany.*

May 20: *A bus picked us up at 3 p.m. and brought us to our ship, [the freighter] "Tacoma." To get to the pier we had to traverse the extensive Port of Hamburg—full of piers, shipyards, repair places, tugboats, etc. We had to undergo all sorts of inspections, including a medical exam. I had to admonish Ernest "for heaven's sake, don't cough!" Well, we were lucky and passed all the examinations and went aboard.*

93

Following A River

May 22 and 23: *We had time to go on land.... We went for a ride to the city of Bremen.... Father [Sally] had some money left, so he went to the Post Office to buy a set of eight Olympic Stamps, which cost one mark—the 1936 Olympics were held in Germany. Remember Jesse Owens? The postal clerk told him he would not sell anything to a Jew. Another incident reinforcing the correctness of our decision to leave Germany.*

May 29: *The White Cliffs of Dover were beautiful to behold.... We could see in the distance some British warships.*

Sally Scheuer, his wife, Hedwig (right), and their son, Ernest. On the left are Sally's sister, Celia Scheuer, and her daughter, Beatrice. This portrait was taken in Germany shortly before the Scheurs began the journey described in Sally's logbook. Courtesy, the Scheuer family.

June 13: *I once read a travel book back in Germany in which the author described going through the Panama Canal as "a ship ride through green meadows."...As far as I [Hedwig] was concerned, as interesting as the canal ride was, I was very depressed being so far away, my folks so far away, and we in the other direction. Of course, in time, we knew how lucky we were to be away.*

July 1: *At 5 p.m. we are in San Diego, the home of the U.S. Pacific fleet. We see quite a few torpedo boats, cruisers, a big aircraft carrier, and many seaplanes.... We went into town in the eve-*

ning. . . . Since we're interested in food stores we saw big markets (for the first time in our lives) where all kinds of edibles can be bought.

July 6: *A San Francisco-based HAPAG [Hamburg-American Steamship Line] agent picked us up and took us to the Immigration Office. The man in charge looked at the attached letter, put it aside and didn't say anything. (I later found out that the letter was something routinely given to people who wore glasses. I guess it said "defective vision.") He asked me whether I spoke English. I said yes. However, during their questioning of me I became very nervous and asked for an interpreter. The HAPAG man volunteered to relay my answers. I was asked my reason for coming to the United States and I told them on account of Hitler's policy against the Jews. The man then looked at the interpreter who had to agree. He might not have liked to admit it, but he was under oath. Then I was asked to swear that I didn't come here to overthrow the United States Government and believe me I could swear that with all my heart and power.*

July 7: *We rode through dense forests. We saw many lakes. As we came closer to Portland the terrain got flatter. The land is very fertile. We saw Mt. Hood, a big snow-capped mountain.*

When we came closer, Ernest, who had taught himself to read the time about two years before, looked at the watch—it was 3 p.m.—and said he was so glad that we would soon be in Portland. Well, we both looked at each other and we didn't know whether we should be glad or sad. We only knew that our travels were coming to an end.

The train pulled into Portland Union Station at 3:35 p.m. Cousin Anselm Boskowitz was there to greet us. (We recognized him from a snapshot he had sent us.)

July 9: *When the news got out that Sally had found a job on his second day in the U.S., many people who had visas for the U.S. came to Portland, hoping to find a job as easily. Eventually they all found work. Being the first family of refugees to come to Portland, we felt that we put it on the map! Since we knew that one has to help the other in paying back Anselm for his kindness (pass it on!)*

Following A River

and we knew first-hand how the situation in Germany was worsening, we played host to many of the later-arriving newcomers. We called them non-swimmers. When they could swim, or at least paddle, they moved on to make room for the next ones.

The above account of one family's flight from Hitler's Germany is typical of thousands of others, and no survey of historical events could match its simple eloquence. As the Scheuers' account suggests, the practice of aiding others to escape the increasingly barbaric tactics of the Nazis became a central preoccupation of Jewish communities across the United States, including Portland.

The Scheuers were fortunate indeed to have fled Germany in the period between 1933 and 1939, for the Nazi concentration camps during this period were still devoted mainly to the retention and torture of political enemies. Jews, while their shops were looted or

Anselm Boskowitz. Courtesy, JHSO.

Referred to in the accompanying narrative as "Cousin Anselm," Anselm Boskowitz was a prominent figure in the Portland Jewish community. His German-born parents, Isaac and Sarah—who owned a general merchandise store in Union, Oregon—sent him to live with his grandmother in Portland when he was 12. Besides playing a major role in the Joint Distribution Committee (for rescuing Jews from Europe), he was a leader in B'nai B'rith and a key figure in establishing the Anti-Defamation League in Oregon and nationally.

Hedwig Scheuer recalls that "Ans was a member of each of the local congregations," and that, upon their arrival in America, he had first taken her and Sally Scheuer to Temple Beth Israel. "We found the services different compared to the more traditional approach that we had been used to," she notes. "Then one evening Ans took Father (Sally) to the Ahavai Sholom and he liked it, so we joined." Clearly, both Temple Beth Israel and Ahavai Sholom benefited by having a man of Boskowitz's vision and stature as a member.

their businesses boycotted, were still allowed an avenue of escape, which often involved payment of a ransom to the German state. In November of 1938, however, the infamous Kristallnacht shattered all this.

Neveh Shalom member Heinz Jacob recalls how, on the morning of November 9, 1938, he biked as usual to his vocational high school in the German city of Breslau, only to be warned to return home as quickly as possible. The tailor to whom he was apprenticed told him that all the synagogues had been destroyed during the night and that most Jewish males had been arrested. Jacob returned to the home of his uncle and aunt, where he was staying at the time. His aunt informed him that his uncle had already been arrested and that the authorities were looking for him and his cousin.

She urged the two boys to take their bikes and ride by a circuitous route to the home of some Gentile friends outside of town. Upon returning to his aunt's house several days later, after things had calmed down, Jacob learned that his father had been incarcerated at Buchenwald. He was able to contact his mother, but could not risk going to find her in the small town of Waldenburg, where she remained, hoping for the early release of her husband.

Amazingly, her hopes were realized and the senior Jacob, because he had actively served in World War I, was released on the promise that he leave Germany. Reunited in Breslau, the Jacob family was again lucky when an opportunity to obtain a visa to Shanghai, China, came their way. "We expected to remain in China for a very short time," Heinz Jacob recalls, "but World War II changed all that. We stayed there for nine long years. Finally, my quota number came up, and I was able to come to the United States."

Upon arriving in Portland, Jacob made arrangements to have his parents join him. But fate intervened when the Chinese communists invaded Shanghai. His parents were forced to flee by night and, since their immigration papers weren't ready, to return to Germany, where they were put in a displaced persons' camp. A month before they were scheduled to come to the United States, Heinz Jacob's father died, and his mother made the long journey to Portland by herself.

Again, this story is representative of thousands of similar ones that begin with Kristallnacht, many of which have far more devastating endings. Between November 9 and 10, 1938, a hundred thousand Jewish men were arrested in Berlin alone. On November 19, 1938, all the Jewish congregations in Portland gathered at Temple

The Portland Jewish community gathers to pray for the victims of Kristallnacht, November 19, 1938. From left: Rabbi Philip Kleinman (Neveh Zedek), Rabbi Joseph Fain (Shaarie Torah), Rabbi Henry Berkowitz (Beth Israel), and Rabbi Charles Sydney (Ahavai Sholom). Courtesy, OHS.

Heinz Jacob (center) and his parents, Siegfried and Alma, in Shanghai about 1934. Courtesy, Heinz Jacob.

1940–1960 / Journeys of Chance

Beth Israel to pray for their fellow Jews and to express their horror at the events of Kristallnacht. Even after Kristallnacht, however, no one could have foreseen or imagined Hitler's "final solution." Like others who watched from afar, Congregations Ahavai Sholom and Neveh Zedek had to piece together the horrible jigsaw of Hitler's incredible plan from conflicting newspaper reports and from the accounts of those who were lucky enough to escape. As the pieces fell together, one priority emerged: to rescue as many people as possible—parents, cousins, strangers—from the impending horror.

Central to this mission was the work of the Oregon Emigre Committee, which had been organized in 1936 by Max Hirsch. With financial support from the Blumauer Fund and the Hebrew Benevolent Society, the Committee raised money and consciousness in an effort to bring German Jews to Portland. Even before the events of Kristallnacht, the Committee had been successful in bringing more than 60 families to Portland and in helping them find work. The latter task was made more difficult by the scarcity of jobs and the general resentment toward immigrants seeking what few jobs were available.

German refugees had other problems during the war years besides finding work and adjusting to a new culture. Being refugees from a country with which the United States was at war made them, in the eyes of officialdom, "enemy aliens." Sally and Hedwig Scheuer's niece, Beatrice Scheuer Chusid, who came to America in 1937 at the age of nine, recalls the curfew imposed on German refugees in Portland. Included in her memorabilia is a letter from the Provost Marshal of the State of Oregon, allowing her and her mother to "be absent from their place of residence after the hour of 8 p.m., Friday, May 22, 1942, for the purpose of attending confirmation services for the said Beatrice Scheurer [sic] at Temple AvaSholom [sic]."

But while the Oregon Emigre Committee provided financial and moral support for the German refugees, much of the task necessarily fell to the individual efforts of people like the Scheuers and their benefactor, Anselm Boskowitz. As early as 1933, shortly after Hitler had seized power, Boskowitz—along with B'nai B'rith Lodge leaders Harry Gevurtz, Alex Miller, Harry Mittleman, and Nathan Weinstein—had been instrumental in boycotting the import of German goods. He now put similar energy into the importing of German refugees.

Following A River

A Tug Toward Tradition: the German Refugees

One of the refugees whom Boskowitz helped in 1939 would become a key figure in congregation Ahavai Sholom in the years to come. This was Karl Bettman, a friend of the Scheuers' who had lived near them in the German town of Bad Nauheim. Bettman's wife, Kaete, was pregnant at the time, and they had just suffered the loss of their three-year-old daughter. After several unsuccessful attempts to find a sponsor for the Bettmans, the Scheuers enlisted the help of Boskowitz.

Ever resourceful, Boskowitz discovered a loophole in the immigration laws that allowed clergymen to come to the United States on a non-quota basis. Undaunted by the fact that Karl Bettman was not a clergyman (though he had served in a lay capacity at his synagogue in Germany), Boskowitz approached the board of Congregation Shaarie Torah and convinced them to draw up a contract offering Bettman a fictitious job as a cleric in the synagogue. On the strength of this ersatz ordination, the Bettmans were able to obtain a visa and come to the United States, where they were soon joined by Karl's son of a previous marriage, Max. Bettman and his wife arrived in Portland in June of 1939 in time for their son Samuel to be born an American citizen in November, one year after Kristallnacht. In that same month, Karl Bettman, unable to assume the non-existent post at Shaarie Torah, obtained the position of sexton at Ahavai Sholom synagogue when the incumbent caretaker fell ill and had to be replaced—thus making Anselm Boskowitz an honest, as well as a deeply moral, man.

The rabbi of Ahavai Sholom at the time of Bettman's appointment as sexton was Charles Sydney. To better understand the extent of Bettman's subsequent influence we have to know something of Rabbi Sydney's role in the history of the congregation.

Rabbi Sydney came to Ahavai Sholom in 1937 after serving eight years as rabbi of a congregation in Freeport, Long Island. He succeeded Rabbi Sandrow, whose youthful vigor and aggressive style, as we have seen, had proved somewhat too progressive for Portland. By contrast, Sydney was, in the words of the *Scribe*, a "tolerant and friendly" man who had little need to get things done in a hurry and who was willing to let others assume leadership and collect credit. His contributions to the Portland community were, again in the words of the *Scribe*, "definite" and "positive": he chaired the Portland Board of Rabbis, served several terms as president of the Portland Zionist Council, was Hillel Counselor at the University of Oregon for more than a decade, and was a member of the boards

1940–1960 / Journeys of Chance

of the Oregon Tuberculosis and Health Association and the Portland Chapter of the National Conference of Christian and Jews. Most significantly, from Ahavai Sholom's point of view, he ushered in an unprecedented period of stability in spiritual leadership, serving the congregation for 14 years, over three times the length of any preceding ordained rabbi. In short, he was a steadying presence, but not as a forceful personality.

Karl Bettman, however, was a forceful personality. He is remembered by some as a large man with a matter-of-fact demeanor and a keen sense of humor. Others remember him as a fine pianist (he brought his piano with him from Germany), a heavy smoker (he could hardly wait until Sabbath services were over to light a cigarette), and as proprietor of the printing shop that he ran to supplement his income from the synagogue (his son Sam took over the shop when Bettman died in 1964 and currently works as a printer in Israel). By all, he is remembered as a man with a single-minded (some might say bullheaded) dedication to the synagogue.

Rabbi Charles Sydney. Courtesy, NS.

Though Bettman undoubtedly ruffled feathers, his status as a refugee from Nazi Germany lent him an aura of authority that precluded outright opposition. Moreover, he was acknowledged as the most educated and knowledgeable of the German refugees who joined Ahavai Sholom in the decade to follow. All of these factors, combined with Rabbi Sydney's tolerant personality, allowed Bettman to emerge as a dominant force in the congregation, serving as executive secretary, reading from the Torah, and on occasion leading services.

The main change that resulted from the influence of Bettman and other German refugees was a shift toward a more traditional, European tone in the congregation. Prior to the influx of German Jews, the trend at Ahavai Sholom was to emulate the liberal practices of the more socially prominent Reform synagogue, Temple Beth Israel. Now, however, came a significant number of very traditional newcomers who had not previously been exposed to the impact of the American environment and who, like Ahavai Sholom's original founders, were intent on preserving their European ways of doing things. While the newcomers were by no means a majority, they became the dominant element in the Sabbath morning service, both in numbers and in influence over the manner in which it was conducted. In contrast to the Friday evening service, which tended to be "Americanized," the Sabbath service took on a distinctly European character under Bettman's leadership.

The ultimate results of these changes were both internal and external: internally, they renewed Ahavai Sholom's sense of identity and underlying strength as a Conservative synagogue; externally, they created a new and stronger image of the congregation in the eyes of the Jewish community. The respect owed to the German refugees and what they represented was extended to the congregation as a whole, which could no longer be perceived as merely "the Polisha shul." Between 1940 and 1950, Ahavai Sholom's membership grew from 200 to 350 families, an unprecedented rate of growth that can be attributed in part to the stability supplied by the presence of Rabbi Sydney and the distinctive character supplied by Karl Bettman and the German refugees.

Bettman was also instrumental in organizing discussion groups for German Jewish emigres to share common problems and to

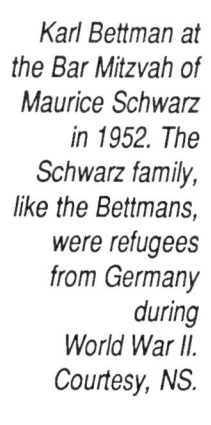

Karl Bettman at the Bar Mitzvah of Maurice Schwarz in 1952. The Schwarz family, like the Bettmans, were refugees from Germany during World War II. Courtesy, NS.

1940–1960 / Journeys of Chance

practice their English. By 1945, when other refugees and survivors of the Holocaust began to arrive, these groups became formally known as the Friendship Club. The club elected officers, held regular monthly meetings, sponsored speakers and cultural events, and helped its members find jobs. Cutting across congregational lines, the Friendship Club played an important role as a support system for German emigres until its dissolution in 1977.

The revitalization that Bettman and the German refugees brought to Ahavai Sholom had its less dramatic counterpart at Neveh Zedek, largely because of the arrival of Rabbi Philip Kleinman and Cantor Joseph Freeman in 1937, the same year that Rabbi Sydney had come to Ahavai Sholom. Born in 1899 in Russia, Cantor Freeman came to America in 1912 to avoid service in the Czar's army. Settling first in New York, he received his cantorial training under some of the leading cantors in that city. He was cantor in a synagogue in Illinois in 1938 when a family member in Portland urged him to come and try for the post left vacant by the death of Abraham Rosencrantz. He received the appointment, and remained with Neveh Zedek for 24 years, right up to the time of the merger with Ahavai Sholom in 1961.

Cantor Joseph Freeman, who served Congregation Neveh Zedek for almost a quarter of a century. Courtesy, Judy Kahn.

Following A River

Rabbi Philip Kleinman, near the end of his life. Courtesy, the Oregonian. *Shown below (third man down from top left) with Neveh Zedek Sunday School children, 1938. Courtesy, JHSO.*

As for Rabbi Kleinman, he introduced a number of innovations oriented toward younger members, including junior services, programs for newly married couples, and a Jewish Boy Scout troop. Ironically, when Neveh Zedek vice-president Sidney Stern interviewed Kleinman in New York in 1937, he wrote back to secretary Adolph Asher that Kleinman "is quite a scholarly and dignified gentleman with only one drawback that I could see and that is his grey hair"—which prompted Stern to wonder whether Kleinman "would appeal to the younger group." Stern also noted that Kleinman seemed "more orthodox" than the rabbis that Neveh Zedek had had in the past. "For instance," Stern explains, "when we had dinner together, he put a 'Yamulki' on his head and said grace after dinner"—adding with admirable broad-mindedness, "However, I don't suppose that that should be held against him." In retrospect, Stern's reservations are somewhat amusing. Though we have no minutes from which to determine the growth rate at Neveh Zedek during the 1940s, other sources suggest that the congregation experienced unprecedented growth during the almost 20 years that Rabbi Kleinman would remain its spiritual leader.

Going with the Times

During the war years, then, both congregations prospered. In addition to stable leadership, the universal effort to support the war worked to bind Portland Jews in a common cause and to diminish bickering over congregational differences. Many members from both Ahavai Sholom and Neveh Zedek served in the armed forces, and many of those at home worked in local war industries such as the Kaiser shipyards, in civil defense, and for the Red Cross. (In the "How Times Have Changed" department, we note a letter of April 1943, from the Red Cross department at Barnes Hospital in Vancouver, Washington, thanking Congregation Ahavai Sholom for its gift to the hospitalized soldiers—cartons of cigarettes!) The B'nai B'rith Lodge, which included members of Ahavai Sholom and Neveh Zedek, sponsored drives for the purchase of war bonds and worked to secure facilities for troops stationed in Portland.

But, as previously noted, by far the most binding force for Portland's Jewish communities was the effort to rescue fellow Jews from their plight in Europe—a plight whose full impact would not be known until the war was over. Eventually, those who arrived included survivors from the extermination and labor camps. Among

Following A River

Jewish servicemen from Oregon and friends, in San Francisco in 1943. Less than a year after this picture was taken, Irv Potter (second from right in back row), a member of a Neveh Zedek family, was killed in action in France. He was one of a number of Portland's Jewish community lost in the war. Courtesy, JHSO.

these was Philip Shuldman, one of Neveh Shalom's current gabbaim (a gabbai was originally a "treasurer," but is now an assistant at the Torah-reading ceremony). Interviewed by Shirley Tanzer in May of 1989, Shuldman supplies us with a remarkable, if grim, Odyssey of survival through sheer self-reliance. Polish by birth, Shuldman was in the Polish army in 1939 when the Poles surrendered to the Germans, and then in several forced labor camps until 1945, when the Americans liberated his camp. Along the way, he tells of anti-Semitism among the Polish soldiers; of his separation from his wife and child, whom he never saw again; of the Ukranian guards who, worse than the Germans, would "every Saturday night get drunk and take off seven, eight people to kill, for fun"; of the prisoner who was blindfolded and shot for asking to observe Rosh Hashanah; of the "nice" German guard who tried to lessen the prisoners' suffering and who "sent over his child to play with the Jewish kids"; of the liberation by the American soldiers, who "did nothing" for the liberated except allow them to stay in the barracks and eat whatever leftover scraps they could find; of four long years in a German hospital recovering from tuberculosis and dysentery.

From the hospital, Shuldman came to America in 1946—first to Toledo, Ohio, where he met and married his present wife, Anne, and then on to Portland, where he and his wife joined Congregation Ahavai Sholom. Shuldman was asked why, with his traditional

1940–1960 / Journeys of Chance

Philip Schuldman as a young man in the Polish army. When the Poles surrendered to the Germans in 1939, Schuldman was taken to a forced labor camp. Courtesy, Philip Schuldman.

background, he didn't join an Orthodox synagogue instead. His reply, given the context of his survival from one of the most extraordinary episodes in recorded human history, speaks volumes: "Yes, but you know, you got to go with the times, I say."

Decisions for Growth: Another New Home

The end of the war found Ahavai Sholom celebrating its 75th anniversary as a fiscally sound and growing congregation. The religious school had reached its highest enrollment ever, 215 children, and was forced to turn away others because of lack of space. To meet this need, the congregation appointed a 75th anniversary building committee to begin a drive for a new religious school and synagogue. At the High Holidays for that year, Hy Nudelman, chairman of the building committee, commented: "In entering the new year our hopes are high that our new synagogue and religious school building will be started before next Yom Kippur." Nudelman's hopes proved a bit too high: six long years of waiting and conflict would pass before construction on the new building would begin, and Nudelman himself would be one of the "casualties" of that conflict.

The main issue of debate and cause of delay arose early and didn't go away. The minutes of June 11, 1946, note, innocently: "The

107

question came up: Should the new facilities be located on the West or East Side?" Once up, the question was not about to go down easily. The contention seems to have hinged on residency. William Toll points out that by 1947 "the American-born children of the Polish Jews who provided the base for Ahavai Shalom now resided in Irvington and the Southeast." Wealthier members, however, including those who held dual memberships in Ahavai Sholom and Beth Israel, tended to live in the West Hills. Since the congregation had decided early that the new religious school should be erected on a lot adjoining the new synagogue, the convenience of transporting children to the new school was clearly a factor in deciding which side of the river to build on. On the other hand, had the need for a new religious school not been as urgent as it was—several minutes from 1947 to 1949 refer to congestion in front of the school and to the fact that the Jewish Community Center was being used to handle the overflow of Sunday School children—the debate might have gone on indefinitely. A number of sites were proposed and rejected—one in the Northeast in August of 1947, and one in the Northwest between Everett and Davis Streets in April of 1948. Though decisions were made to obtain options on both properties, both were ultimately rejected by the building committee.

As Congregation Ahavai Sholom continued to haggle over the location of its new home, however, an event that the entire Jewish world had long awaited was on the verge of becoming a reality. On May 14, 1948, the British troops departed Palestine and Jews there listened as David Ben-Gurion proclaimed the independent state of Israel. That evening, the Israelis celebrated the long-awaited founding of their homeland. The next morning they took their places at the front lines to defend it against five separate Arab armies that swooped down on them from all directions.

News of the Israeli War of Independence (1948-49) could hardly dampen the jubilation that swept the Jewish world on hearing that they had a homeland at last. For Jews everywhere it was the fulfillment of a hope that had permeated Jewish thinking since the earliest days of the Diaspora—that they would someday return to Zion. For members of the Portland Jewish community it was confirmation that their years of praying and giving had not been in vain. And for younger members, who must at the time have been mystified by the intensity of the celebration, it would become a symbol of Jewish unity and pride. As Neveh Shalom member Gussie Reinhardt put it, the news of the founding of the state of Israel was like "a light from heaven."

In the afterglow of that light, Congregation Ahavai Sholom finally managed to reach a decision about its new synagogue, though not a particularly wise one. The minutes for October 7, 1948, note that "It was decided in the form of a motion that the Congregational building be erected on the present site." How, after all the debate about a new location, this surprising decision came about is not clear, but March of 1949 found the building plans drawn up by the firm of Dugan, Heims, and Cain and approved by the Portland City Council. The cost of the new building would be $210,000, to be paid through a loan from the First National Bank of $100,000 "under certain circumstances" and a fund-raising effort for the remainder.

Despite the obvious space limitations, the intention to build on the old site persisted for almost two years while the fund-raising proceeded. Then, on January 24, 1951, the minutes report a discussion of "the possibility of switching the building plan to the Horenstein property, located at SW 13th and Market Streets." The half-block at 13th and Market had a number of advantages: it was considerably larger than the old site, and it was directly across the street from the Jewish Community Center, which the congregation had been using for some time as a secondary religious school. These advantages were apparently not lost on the building committee. Less than a month later the congregation decided to secure an option on the Horenstein property and on June 3 decided to buy it.

Between securing an option on the Horenstein property and actually buying it, the congregation learned a disturbing bit of news—namely, that they had not been a bona fide congregation for the previous six years. It seems that the officers of Ahavai Sholom had overlooked the State of Oregon statute that required filing Power of Attorney, with the result that "said Congregation was dissolved automatically December 31, 1945, pursuant to Oregon Law." The oversight was brought to their attention when they attempted to execute a mortgage for the erection of the new synagogue, and was hastily rectified. Whether the six-year status as a legal non-entity subconsciously affected the congregation's drawn-out debate about where to locate the new synagogue is a matter for psychologists, not historians, to determine.

By September of 1951 the congregation was considering various contractors' bids, and on October 8 it accepted the bid of Ross, Hammond & Co. March of the following year found the building half completed, and on May 25 the cornerstone was laid for the

Following A River

Laying of the cornerstone for Ahavai Sholom's 13th Street Shul, May 25, 1952. From left to right, Erwin "Ike" Davis, president; Philip Weinstein, co-chairman of Sunday Schools; Max Lesman, member of the building committee; Mayor Dorothy McCullogh Lee; and Rabbi Ralph Weissberger. Rabbi Weissberger would resign before the year was out. Below, the 13th Street Shul. Courtesy, NS.

building that would be Ahavai Sholom's final place of worship before it merged with Neveh Zedek in 1961. The Park Avenue building was sold to the First Christian Church and was later to be used as a gymnasium by Portland State University. In 1978, after a valiant but unsuccessful attempt to save it by having it registered as an historic landmark, the wood-framed structure on Park Avenue was demolished.

What the sparse entries in the minutes fail to convey are the hard feelings that accompanied the choice of location for the new synagogue. A number of families—including that of Hy Nudelman, original chairman of the building committee—left the congregation, and the subject would remain a sore spot for several years after the new synagogue was completed. The minutes do reveal that on June 14, 1951, 11 days after an agreement was reached to purchase the Horenstein property, Rabbi Sydney resigned. Whether these two events are related in any way other than chronological coincidence must remain a matter of conjecture. Whatever the circumstances, Rabbi Sydney departed in September of that year, having received a parting gift of $5,000 for his years of service. Whether he or someone else performed the High Holiday services for that year is not clear. A cryptic entry for August 23, 1951, mentions a decision to hire a Rabbi Nathan Gaynor of Alexandria, Virginia, at the salary of $9,000, plus $1,000 moving expenses, for one year. This is the only reference to Gaynor in the minutes, and other sources strongly indicate that he never actually came to Portland. What we do know is that on January 9, 1952, the congregation hired Rabbi Ralph Weissberger of New York to occupy the pulpit at a salary of $10,000 a year—though, as fate would have it, Rabbi Weissburger was to resign before the year was out.

It was in the midst, then, of considerable congregational turmoil that, on September 7, 1952, the new building was dedicated. Within a month, Rabbi Weissberger would resign and the new, beautifully panelled pulpit would be empty. To those with any knowledge of the congregation's history, it must have seemed that Ahavai Sholom was about to lose what stability it had gained during the past decade and to revert to its old pattern of disposable rabbis. December of 1952 found the congregation interviewing various religious leaders, little knowing what a profound effect their choice would have on the future of the congregation.

Following A River

A Fortuitous Find: Rabbi Joshua Stampfer

Since mid-century, two events must stand out as singularly formative to the current character of Congregation Neveh Shalom. One is the merger between Ahavai Sholom and Neveh Zedek in 1961. The other is the hiring, in 1953, of Rabbi Joshua Stampfer.

Joshua Stampfer was born in Jerusalem in 1921, the son and grandson of rabbis. His grandfather on his mother's side had been the Chief Rabbi of Jerusalem, and his great-grandfather on his father's side was noted for traveling by foot from Hungary to the land of Israel, where he founded the settlement of Petah Tikvah.

Rabbi Joshua Stampfer. Courtesy, the Stampfer family.

Because great-grandfather Stampfer had spent time in the United States at a time when American naturalization laws were lax, the next three generations of Stampfers were registered as American citizens, even though none of them had been to the U.S. When, in 1922, the naturalization laws were changed to require residency, Stampfer's father decided that he wanted to retain his American citizenship. Consequently, he brought the family to this country, establishing themselves first in Chicago and then in Akron, Ohio, where Joshua Stampfer grew up.

After graduating from the University of Chicago and being ordained at the Jewish Theological Seminary of America in 1949, Stampfer took up the pulpit of Congregation Tifereth Israel in Lincoln, Nebraska. When asked in a 1980 interview why he decided

1940–1960 / Journeys of Chance

to come to Portland after four years in Nebraska, Rabbi Stampfer replied with typically quiet humor: "Well, probably the most striking impression was that I came to visit in January and came home with a bunch of camelias. I figured that any place that would have camelias in January was better than Nebraska."

The camelias were long gone when Stampfer arrived in June of 1953 with his wife, Goldie, and their three young sons, Shaul, Meir, and Noam. The boys immediately won the hearts of the congregation, which was not accustomed to having children included in its rabbinical bargains. Nor did it take the congregation long to recognize what a prize it had in Goldie Stampfer. She was soon active in the Sisterhood, writing program material for both local and national distribution, and she would eventually become the only rabbi's wife to serve as president of the Northwest Branch of the National

Rabbi Joshua Stampfer, Goldie Stampfer, and their three sons, (from left) Noam, Shaul, and Meir, shortly after their arrival in Portland in 1953. Later, Nehama, born in 1956, and Elana, born in 1963, would complete the Stampfer family. Courtesy, the Stampfer family.

Following A River

Goldie Stampfer (seated, second from left) and the Pacific Northwest Delegation of the National Women's League at its convention in 1972, when she was president of the Northwest Branch. Courtesy, Goldie Stampfer.

Women's League--this in addition to, at various times over the years, teaching in the religious school, being an active member of most of the Portland Jewish women's organizations, and serving as president of the Portland chapter of Hadassah, a post which she currently holds.

As for the Rabbi Stampfer, the most immediate task facing him upon his arrival in 1953 was tending to a series of weddings that had backed up because of the lack of a rabbi to perform them. He recalls performing four weddings in one day during his first week in Portland: "For a while I wasn't sure what wedding I was performing. I had a list in front of me—number one, number two, number three. I didn't know the people."

Rabbi Stampfer lost little time, however, in getting to know his congregation of just over 200 families and in assessing its needs. The leadership at the time consisted of the executive secretary, Karl Bettman; Treasurer Saul Wax; President Erwin "Ike" Davis; Hy Solko, Philip Weinstein, and Maurice Sussman, all of whom were later to become presidents; along with primary financial supporters such as Sam Zidell. Despite this fairly broad and active leadership, two characteristics of Ahavai Sholom soon became evident to Stampfer: first, it was a congregation divided amongst itself, with considerable hard feelings remaining about the controversy over East Side versus West Side; secondly, it was a congregation with very little interest in extending its stature within the community or in broadening its exposure to cultural influences. On the other hand,

Rabbi Stampfer soon discovered that, presented with initiatives for various programs, the congregation proved to be consistently supportive and enthusiastic.

Among the innovations that Rabbi Stampfer introduced during his first year at Ahavai Sholom were the establishment of a nursery school (which would eventually become the current Foundation School), the publication of the Ahavai Sholom *Chronicle*, for the reporting of congregational news, and the introduction of a junior congregational service. He also initiated what would become a long tradition of inviting outside speakers to address the congregation on cultural, political, and social topics. On November 13, 1953, Senator Richard Neuberger spoke to the congregation on "Writing for Children," an event that included an exhibit of children's books of Jewish interest and a social hour hosted by the Sisterhood. (The *Chronicle* page that describes this event also announces a talk by Rabbi Stampfer on the theme, "Rest and Grow Rich, the Case for the Five-Day Week"—further evidence that the new rabbi quickly grasped the temperament of his Northwest audience!)

In the years that would follow, Rabbi Stampfer would become not only the major force in his congregation, but a prominent educational figure in the community and beyond. Besides being an adjunct Associate Professor at Portland State University from 1960 to 1982, Rabbi Stampfer has initiated and fostered educational programs that have influenced Jewish life in the entire Pacific Northwest. High on any list of Jewish educational resources is the Institute for Judaic Studies, founded by Stampfer in 1983. Before that time, Portland was the largest city in the United States that did not have a program in Judaic studies. When Portland State University closed its Middle East Study Center in 1982, Stampfer approached the presidents of Portland State University and Reed College and proposed the founding of an institute that would provide the greater Portland community with programs in Judaica. The Institute for Judaic Studies, housed in Portland State University's Division of Continuing Education building, continues to fulfill its defined role as an "academic networker" for persons interested in pursuing Judaic studies. Other institutions that owe their existence to Stampfer's imagination and energy include the Jewish Historical Society of Oregon, the Oregon Holocaust Resource Center, and Camp Solomon Schechter, which we will be visiting in the next chapter. From the time of his arrival in 1953, he has continued to raise

Following A River

the spiritual and intellectual sights of the congregation and, by doing so, to raise the stature of the congregation in the eyes of the community and even the country.

In short, then, the coming together in 1953 of a handsome new building and an energetic new rabbi proved to be fortuitous indeed for Congregation Ahavai Sholom. The combination quickly attracted new members, especially families with young children who could benefit from the emerging educational advantages of the congregation's fine new school wing, its new nursery school, and its new camp. By contrast, Congregation Neveh Zedek, although it boasted the handsome stone building on S.W. Sixth Avenue, had almost no facilities for children and was becoming primarily an older community. For classrooms to accommodate what children it had, the congregation used corners of balconies and small storerooms. Rabbi Kleinman had just retired, and while young, active rabbis such as Norman Siegel and Jack Segal did their best to revitalize the congregation, the lack of younger families and the lack of space presented insurmountable obstacles. Even as the synagogue property, being located downtown, became more and more valuable, it became less and less usable for a congregation with any desire for growth.

Despite the disparity in the age levels of most members from Neveh Zedek and Ahavai Sholom, Portland's two conservative congregations had much in common. Still, no one was about to suggest yet another attempt at a merger, if indeed the idea even occurred. As for what might have happened, Rabbi Stampfer conjectures: "I imagine that things would have gone along with the usual status quo and inertia until vast changes took place in the community itself, in the city itself." As for what did happen, one such change in the city indeed intervened: the building of a new freeway. As fate would have it, Ahavai Sholom's controversial synagogue, not yet 10 years old, was now standing directly in the path of civic progress. As the reality of this situation became more imminent, people in both camps began to think in terms of a merger. Why not build a new synagogue elsewhere that would meet everyone's needs and use the resources of both congregations? Why not, indeed? The question hung like a wrecking ball, waiting to do its decisive, devisive work.

Opposite: Worship services at Ahavai Sholom (top) and Neveh Zedek shortly before the two congregations merged in 1961. Courtesy, NS.

1961-1989
The Necessary And The Possible

The necessary is always possible.
—Hugo von Hofmannsthal

A Difficult Union

Rivers wear many faces. On a calm, cloudless day, it is hard to imagine that a serene stream was once a furious torrent. Similarly, the visitor gazing at the face of Neveh Shalom's synagogue on Peaceful Lane today would be hard put to imagine the turmoil that broiled up around the choice of this site or the design of this building.

The practical advantages of merging Congregations Ahavai Sholom and Neveh Zedek were compelling from the start. Both synagogues were Conservative and both stood to gain by joining forces. Ahavai Sholom was losing its building on S.W. Thirteenth and Market to the proposed freeway and would have to build a new one in any case. The merger was a logical and desirable way to increase its membership and resources. Neveh Zedek was losing its membership to attrition, having shrunk from over 300 families to 170 at the time of the proposed merger. More importantly, the average age of the membership was 60, and the Sunday School was not attracting new families with young children. Merging with the larger, younger, and more active synagogue promised to benefit the existing membership in every way.

But practical advantages are often lost sight of in the heat of emotional attachments. For many members of Neveh Zedek, the proposed merger represented not merely the loss of a synagogue in which they had worshipped for half a century, but the loss of identity as well. The expression most often used by those who recall the members' sentiments at the time is that they were afraid of being "swallowed up." It is a strong phrase, one that calls to mind Woody Allen's observation, "The lion and the lamb shall lie down together, but the lamb won't get much sleep."

Seeing themselves as becoming the lesser partner in an unequal marriage, the members of Neveh Zedek were not about to agree to the nuptials without resistance. First, there was the question of the "dowry," Neveh Zedek's "Upkeep Fund," whose primary purpose was the maintenance of the congregation's cemetery. Despite assurances that the congregations' two cemeteries would be maintained as separate corporations, the emotional aura surrounding the traditional importance of the cemetery in Jewish life left many members reluctant even to listen to talk of a merger. In addition, as in many modern marriages, there was the issue of changing the name of either congregation. Louis Gevurtz, for one, was against changing the name of Ahavai Sholom, and we can assume that some Neveh Zedek members felt even more strongly about losing their name along with their identity. Also, there was the important question of who would be rabbi and cantor of the newly formed congregation, since each congregation had its own, and supporting two rabbis and two cantors was clearly impractical.

These assorted psychological and practical problems were in themselves substantial enough to cast a shadow on any attempt to merge the two congregations. To fully appreciate the reluctance of Neveh Zedek, however, we need to remember that the congregation had just gone through an aborted attempt to build a new synagogue on the East Side and possibly to merge with yet another congregation, Shaarie Torah. That attempt, begun in 1959, had resulted in a series of disturbing phone calls to Rabbi Jack Segal, beginning with one from an unidentified woman who spurted out "You dirty Jew!" and hung up. (Perhaps topping this insulting call was one that Rabbi Segal received a year later when his weekly radio program, "The Open Ark," was interrupted by a campaign speech by Richard Nixon. A member of the congregation called and complained: "Rabbi, I didn't enjoy your program this week. I don't like it when you discuss politics.") At least a dozen people from Neveh Zedek, including President Si Cohn and several others who lived near the proposed site on N.E. 35th and Klickitat, received similar calls. Ap-

1961–1989 / The Necessary and the Possible

Rabbi Jack Segal, who served Congregation Neveh Zedek from 1958 until the time of the merger in 1961. Observing Rabbi Segal as he cuts a challa is his wife, Toby. Courtesy, Judy Kahn.

parently, these calls were the work of a few bigots who didn't want a synagogue in their neighborhood of expensive homes, but the effect on the congregation was understandably traumatic.

An article in the *Oregonian* for July 15, 1959, notes that the City Council was postponing its settlement of the "bitter dispute" over whether the congregation should be permitted to build the proposed $400,000 synagogue. The request for the delay had come from President Si Cohn, the Multnomah County Clerk at the time, who reported that "some members of his congregation question whether the church [sic] should be built at the proposed new location in light of the neighborhood objections." In the end, bigotry had its day and the congregation decided to retract its offer on the 39,600 square-foot site. An ensuing law suit was ultimately settled in the congregation's favor, but not without leaving a bitter taste in everyone's mouth about new synagogues and proposed mergers. In light of this distasteful affair, the surprising thing is not that congregation Neveh Zedek members resisted the merger with Ahavai Sholom less than a year later, but that they were willing to even consider it at all.

But consider it they did. To address the proposed merger, President Si Cohn of Neveh Zedek and President Louis Rosenberg of Ahavai Sholom appointed a joint committee that met for the first time on September 6, 1960. The committee consisted of Louis Gevurtz, Hy Solko, Maurice Sussman, and Philip Weinstein from Ahavai Sholom, and Harry Jackson, Abraham "English" Rosenberg, Ben Steinberg, and Dave Weiner from Neveh Zedek. A factor in the ultimate outcome of the series of meetings that followed was that

Neveh Zedek's English Rosenberg and Ahavai Sholom president Louis Rosenberg were brothers and that their roots were in Neveh Zedek. But even with this familial bond across congregational lines, English Rosenberg recalls, the meetings generated a "general uproar" among the members of Neveh Zedek congregation, with "lots of arguments and even bitterness in some quarters."

Committee member Dave Weiner notes that almost none of the arguments resulted from differences in ritual, though these were discussed: "We said, 'Ahavai Sholom has an organ, but we can live with that. They have singing, but we can live with that. They have Gentiles in the choir. That can be corrected.'" The points of controversy, rather, were mainly psychological, based in great part on the traditionally fierce independence of the Neveh Zedek faction, and what may have been perceived as a patronizing attitude on the part of the Ahavai Sholom representatives. As for the degree of bitterness that these meetings excited in the older membership of Neveh Zedek, Cele Blumenthal's description of the process is revealing. Even in an interview in 1984, 23 years after the merger, she recalled the "dirty politics" by which "a few people railroaded that thing through," adding: "Before we knew it, it was signed, sealed, and delivered."

If there was any railroading, however, it was with a fairly slow train. The meetings went on for six months before the matter was finally put to a vote of the two congregations. Dave Weiner recalls that when Neveh Zedek voted on the proposed merger, President Si Cohn was in ill health and on the verge of losing control of the meeting. As vice-president, Weiner took over and reminded the members that they had voted down every other attempt to improve or revitalize the congregation, and that this might well be their last chance. After numerous questions and much heated debate, the proposed merger was put to a vote. It passed, whereupon a significant minority of those present left the meeting, some of them not to return.

At Ahavai Sholom, meanwhile, the outcome of the voting was almost a foregone conclusion. From the outset, Rabbi Stampfer and President Louis Rosenberg had seen the merger as a means of strengthening both the Conservative Movement and the congregation. Rosenberg—Ahavai Sholom's last president and Neveh Shalom's first—was highly esteemed by both congregations and, avoiding any factionalism within Ahavai Sholom, provided a steadying hand throughout the merger discussions. Moreover, since

1961–1989 / The Necessary and the Possible

Congregation Ahavai Sholom was going to have to move somewhere to avoid the new freeway, the prospect of leaving their present synagogue was not the emotional issue that it was at Neveh Zedek. In short, Ahavai Sholom had nothing to lose, and much to gain, always a good position from which to be bargaining.

After approving the merger, the next step was to decide on a name for the new congregation. The obvious choices were "Ahavai Zedek" or "Neveh Shalom." Rabbi Stampfer recalls that he had always been somewhat embarrassed by the fact that "Ahavai" was incorrect (the proper transliteration of the Hebrew word would have been "Ohavai") and that he was therefore strongly in favor of naming the new synagogue "Neveh Shalom." That sentiment won the day, and on April 4, 1961, the joint committee of the two congregations unanimously voted that the "Dwelling of Righteousness" and the "Lover of Peace" would hereafter be called "Neveh Shalom," the "Dwelling of Peace."

Finding a site for the dwelling, however, proved anything but peaceful. As the minutes note, the East Side versus West Side issue surfaced once again, causing "much high blood pressure." Members who lived on the East Side naturally favored a site near their neighborhoods, whereas Rabbi Stampfer and others felt that building on the East Side would be "disastrous" to the future of the congregation, since the movement of the Jewish population was decidedly to the West Side, but away from the downtown area. Still a third group, including the original building committee, had in mind "locating the new building in the core of the city." A related and equally volatile issue was the matter of transportation. Many felt on principle that the new site should be accessible by bus—this in spite of the fact that very few of the members depended on public transportation as a means of getting to services. As quickly as chairman Dan Davis and the building committee could review and suggest a site, some vocal group of members found ample reasons for objecting to it.

Louis Rosenberg, president of Ahavai Sholom, 1960-1961. A beloved leader, Rosenberg played a key role in the merger negotiations. Courtesy, NS.

This was no less true of the Dosch Road site that was ultimately chosen, which was a considerable distance from either the East Side or from the core of the city. For one thing, it was not on a bus route, so that members without cars would have difficulty getting to it. Arnold Cogan, a civil engineer and future president of the congregation, was also quick to point out that the combination of underground springs and the downward slope of the Dosch Road property would very likely cause serious drainage problems. (This prophecy proved all too true. In 1978, the congregation found itself with a sinking parking lot and, eventually, a natural lake. Bus transportation was in place by then, but President Norman Wapnick wryly observed that "the congregation may never know how close they came to having to take a boat to services!" Despite the drawbacks of the Dosch Road site, however, the undeniable advantages were that it was large and reasonably priced—13 acres for $50,000.

And so, on April 29, 1962, members from the newly-merged congregation met in the old sanctuary of Ahavai Sholom to vote on this most recently proposed site for their dwelling of peace. Dave Weiner, who had been newly appointed as "3rd vice-president" (a step just above the two "honorary vice-presidents"), has described that meeting as "a scene that shouldn't be remembered." And apparently it isn't—at least not with anything like objectivity. What people do remember is the tone. English Rosenberg recalls it as "a terrible meeting," marked by much "noise, bitterness, and animosity." Jerry Stern, who was also at the meeting, has contended that the goal of the meeting was to "shove the site down the congregation's throat." Arnold Cogan describes the meeting as "the most unfortunate mistake in a series of mistakes," noting that many felt it was held in the sanctuary for the explicit purpose of intimidating people from speaking out. When that purpose collided head-on with what Dave Weiner refers to as "an organized revolt led by Dave Weinstein," the outcome was nothing less than mayhem. Fritzie Sussman Campf finally rose, a female lighthouse in a tossing sea of floundering men-o'-war, and roundly chastised the men for their behavior and language in a house of worship. This brought the group to a vote, if not to its senses, and the proposed site was rejected by a vote of 131 to 118.

Having lost the vote, along with $500 that they had put down on the property as earnest money, the original building committee had had enough, and a second committee was formed under the chairmanship of Lou Olds. Sites were reviewed, discussions, were

1961–1989 / The Necessary and the Possible

held, arms were twisted, and, in the meantime, life went on. Those who remember this year—1962—especially recall the devastating Columbus Day storm that ushered in Succoth. When the congregation's lovingly constructed Succoth booth was one of the few structures to survive the storm unscathed, the Neveh Shalom *Chronicle* hailed the fact as a "miracle." Though services had to be held by candlelight, the survival of the Succah rendered the holiday one of the bright spots in a stormy year.

By February of 1963, the upshot of all the renewed activity was that the second building committee came up with the same recommendation as the first committee. By this time, however, the amount of property available on the Dosch Road site had shrunk from 13 acres to eight acres and the price had ballooned from $50,000 to $60,000. Still, the terms were considerably more reasonable than others that were available, and the committee urged that the congregation accept the terms before things got worse. Once again the Dosch Road site was presented to the membership for a vote. This time, Rabbi Stampfer, who had been persuaded to observe the earlier meeting from the balcony, refused to take a back seat and instead took the pulpit to make a plea for approval of the site. Reason prevailed, and the site on Dosch Road was approved by a vote of 205 to 91. Neveh Shalom was one step nearer to having a new home.

*Cantor Chaim Feifel (left) and Rabbi Joshua Stampfer celebrating Succoth by candlelight during the 1962 Columbus Day storm. Cantor Feifel served Congregation Neveh Shalom from 1962 to 1967. He currently resides in Zihron Yaakov, Israel.
Courtesy, NS.*

Following A River

Building for the Future

But there were unexpected stumbling blocks still to come, the most memorable of which was an event that necessitated some creative adjustments on the part of the newly formed congregation. At noon on Saturday, March 21, 1964, the flat roof of Ahavai Sholom synagogue collapsed because of an accumulation of rainwater. Custodian Major Pruitt, who was in the building at the time with his five-year-old daughter, Viola, recalls that a Bat Mitzvah scheduled for that morning had been cancelled, noting that had congregants been using the social hall at the time, a number of people would almost certainly have been killed.

As it was, Pruitt and his daughter were standing in the auditorium, where the main damage occurred, when they heard a noise "like thunder or an earthquake." The next thing Pruitt knew, he was being hit by cascading water and being knocked back against a wall. He lost sight of his daughter momentarily, but found her huddled against another wall, unharmed. After the water, came plasterboard, heavy wooden beams, and structural underpinnings. Finally, the bursting roof crashed down and through an overhead storage area, carrying a number of folding chairs. When he had regained his composure, Pruitt called Executive Secretary Karl Bettman and reported that there was "water in the synagogue." Bettman, failing to comprehend the situation, replied matter-of-factly: "Well, don't call me—call a plumber." (Bettman, incidentally, was never to see the new synagogue, for he died three months after the incident involving the collapse of the roof.)

When the full extent of the damage was realized, several members conjectured that a drain on the roof had plugged, allowing water to collect and overload the roof structure. A less plausible explanation was that the roof had been weakened by all the shouting that had gone on over the proposed site for the new synagogue—suggesting that the collapse may have involved symbolic as well as hydraulic weight. Whatever the cause of the near-disastrous event, it soon became clear that the synagogue and religious school were unusable. From the time of the roof collapse until the new building was completed, therefore, services for the merged congregation were held at the old Neveh Zedek synagogue, while the religious school classes shifted to St. Helen's Private Episcopal School Hall and elsewhere.

By this time, a capital funds drive under the co-chairmanship of Nat Barocas, Leon Feldstein, and English Rosenberg was well under way. One of the few controversial elements introduced into the drive

With the collapse of the synagogue roof in 1964, Neveh Shalom came perilously close to losing one of its congregational treasures, Major Pruitt, shown inspecting the damage with his daughter, Viola. Courtesy, Amy Goldstein.

Major Pruitt was hired as caretaker of Congregation Ahavai Shalom in 1954 when his job in the dining car department of the Union Pacific Railroad was cut because of declining business. Since that time, Pruitt has become so indispensable to the congregational life that no job title seems any longer to fit. He has mastered the complex Jewish calendar and maintains all the congregation's Yahrzeit records; he orders the memorial plaques, using the Hebrew printed form letters; as the Mashgiach (Kosher supervisor) he makes sure that every food that enters the synagogue meets the Kashrut code; as the wedding consultant, he directs all the wedding rehearsals in the synagogue; and as the major-domo at all synagogue events, he sees that all the ritual needs are met. "Major is a wonderful human being with an extraordinary memory," Rabbi Stampfer observes. "And the children flock around him. They adore him."

In 1969, when Pruitt completed fifteen years of service to the congregation, he was offered a trip to Israel as a gift. He regretfully turned it down because he absolutely refuses to fly in a plane. "When they lay a railroad line to Israel," the former Union Pacific employee noted, "I'll be happy to visit."

Lou Olds (left), chairman of Neveh Shalom's second building committee and Abraham "English" Rosenberg, who spurred the capital funds drive. Courtesy, NS.

A fund-raising meeting for the synagogue on Dosch Road. Karl Bettman, seated left, did not live to see the move to the new synagogue. At the podium are Norman Wapnick (front) and Kurt Hamburger, both of whom later served as presidents of Neveh Shalom. Courtesy, NS.

was the hiring of a professional fundraiser from New York, whom a number of members felt was too aggressive for their tastes. Still, with monies from the sale of Neveh Zedek synagogue and compensation from the State of Oregon for the Ahavai Sholom property, combined with help from the very resourceful Sisterhood, raising money for the new building proved to be one of the smoother operations of the entire merger. Fritzie Campf, president of the Sisterhood at the time, recalls it as an exciting and enjoyable process.

Coming up with a design that would meet the approval of all parties involved was, however, a different matter. Undoubtedly, any design would have been controversial in some quarters, and the one finally selected, by the architectural firm of Percy and Lathrop, was no exception. Though Rabbi Stampfer, among others, still harbors regrets about certain elements of the design that were necessitated by financial considerations—the flat roof, the large pillars and low ceilings in the social hall—he feels that the building satisfactorily meets the main criterion of looking like a synagogue and nothing else. Some felt, however, that the huge reproduction of the Decalogue that dominates the facade of the building was oversized and gaudy, reminiscent perhaps of a drive-in movie screen showing credits for Cecil B. De Mille's "The Ten Commandments." This impression was modified somewhat by tasteful and proportionate landscaping, and those who championed the prominent facade could later take some satisfaction in the fact that the building, because of its high visibility from the air, became an airlane signal for planes heading for Portland International Airport. Even to this day, however, the architecture of the building remains a subject of occasional discussion, if not controversy.

But despite the controversy, despite the reluctance, despite the fears, the new synagogue was completed, a tribute to everyone involved and to the spirit of endurance that is the hallmark of the Jewish faith. That spirit was celebrated at the dedication ceremonies in a moving cantata composed by Richard Moffatt and performed jointly by the Neveh Shalom and Portland State College choirs. Called "Jerusalem," the choral narrative, written by Rabbi Stampfer, closes with the traditional blessing for joyous occasions:

> Blessed art Thou, O Lord our God,
> King of the Universe, who hast
> Kept us in life and sustained us
> And brought us to this moment.

Following A River

The "moment," in the context of the narrative, was Israel Independence Day, but to all who were present at that performance of March 6, 1965, the moment was also the finalizing of a union that had taken 70 years to consummate, the joining of Portland's two Conservative congregations under the roof a a new and single building.

Though some hard feelings lingered, especially among the older members of the former Neveh Zedek congregation, the transition to a unified congregation was accomplished through compromise, general good will, and the mere passage of time. Rabbi Stampfer, because of his seniority, stayed on as the spiritual leader of the new congregation. The two cemeteries and their funds were held and administered as separate entities. The daily minyan, a long and treasured tradition for former Neveh Zedek members, was preserved, and organ music was eventually eliminated. Most importantly, perhaps, the halls of the new religious school rang with the irrepressible enthusiasm of the young, a sign to all that the future held a promise of vitality and growth.

Neveh Shalom synagogue on Peaceful Lane, off Dosch Road. Courtesy, NS.

130

1961–1989 / The Necessary and the Possible

A happy day in December, 1964: the first wedding at Neveh Shalom Synagogue. Betty Lynn Fendel and Albert Menashe. Courtesy, NS.

A sad day in February, 1965: the destruction of the building that had been Congregation Neveh Zedek's place of worship for 50 years. Courtesy, OHS.

Following A River

The first Bat Mitzvah in Neveh Shalom's new sanctuary, February 20, 1965: Francine Hodes and mother, Shirley Hodes.

Appropriately, this first Bat Mitzvah involved a family whose roots go as far back as those of any in the congregation. It all started in Lithuania in 1884, when Max Swirsky married his cousin Fruma Swirsky, sister of later Ahavai Sholom President Sam Swirsky (1869-1951). Max and Fruma had four children before emigrating to America and shortening the family name to Swire: Kate, who married Joseph Maxwell Greenberg; George, who married Preva Sax; Rose, who married Sol Lesman; and Sarah, who married Michael Hodes. George and Preva Swire had a daughter, Marcia, and a son, Mel. Sarah and Michael Hodes had a daughter, Blossom, and a son, Stan, who married Shirley Minevitch, pictured above with their daughter, Francine Hodes (now Abolofia). The first generation of Portland Swires are shown in the 1910 portrait below. From left: Rose (1889-1958), George (1894-1973), Fruma (1862-1952), Sarah (1897-   ), Max (1860-1935), and Kate (1884-1940). Courtesy, Marcia Weinsoft.

1961–1989 / The Necessary and the Possible

At the time of the dedication of the new synagogue, the enrollment in the religious school of Neveh Shalom was at an all-time high of 542 students. This figure reflects several factors, including the additional space in the new building and the joining of teaching staffs from the two synagogues. But it reflects as well the dedicated work of the various principals--especially Harriet Steinberg and Toinette Menashe--who would carry on the fine work begun by Grayce Gumbert in the fifties. Besides developing an outstanding core elementary school curriculum, the religious school teachers and administrators organized a number of innovative programs after school on Sundays, including a drama program, Hebrew classes, and other special interest groups. Activities also included picnics, school-wide celebrations, Shabbatons, and Bible quizzes.

The Foundation School, established in September of 1954, marked the beginning of Neveh Shalom's abiding commitment to early childhood education. Based on the philosophy that the seeds of Jewish learning are planted at an early age, the "Nursery School" (as it was fondly called in the early years) was launched at Ahavai

Education: Hallmark of the Stampfer Era

Rabbi Joshua Stampfer and the 1969 Consecration class. The teacher at far right is Eleanor Horenstein. Courtesy, NS.

Following A River

Sholom under the direction of Jackie Merrin. In the late fifties and throughout the sixties, Ethel Suher and Irma Keller continued to guide the school, seeing it through the move to Peaceful Lane. In the early seventies, Leah Rubin assumed the role of director that she still holds. The original program of the nursery school expanded as more women entered the workplace and the need for day care increased. Currently licensed by the State of Oregon and the Children's Services Division, the Foundation School of Neveh Shalom has earned its wings as one of Portland's finest preschools.

Yet another form of education for members of Neveh Shalom is the United Synagogue Youth (USY) chapter for high school students. Founded in October of 1953, the group modestly chose the name "Rishonim" (Number One), reflecting that it was the largest synagogue-affiliated youth group in the Pacific Northwest. While USY programs have a strong religious element, the emphasis of activities is on social service rather than academic development. Many USY members have gone on to take an active role in synagogue life. Mark Ail, for example, who was the USY president in 1966, went on to become president of the congregation twenty years later, the only USY youth to achieve that distinction thus far.

Behind all of these innovations in education has been the guiding influence of Joshua Stampfer. And this is to say nothing of the less formal educational projects that Stampfer has initiated over the years: the study groups in private homes, the discussion forums for downtown businessmen, the tours to Israel for students at Portland State University. In addition, the Stampfer home has itself become an educational, as well as social, extension of the synagogue. For over 20 years, the Leader's Training Fellowship—a group for motivated youngsters with leadership potential—met in the Stampfer home on Saturday afternoons.

In short, like Julius Eckman, Rabbi Stampfer has placed education of the young as the cornerstone of his work (Stampfer's biography of Eckman, published in 1989, reveals other strong affinities between the two religious leaders). No single program initiated by Stampfer more clearly illustrates this commitment than Camp Solomon Schechter. Standing as a symbol of Stampfer's unique contribution to the congregation that he has served for 35 years, as well as to Jewish life in the Pacific Northwest, Camp Solomon Schechter deserves special attention here.

It was while serving as counselor at Brandeis Camp Institute in 1943 that Stampfer met his future wife, Goldie Goncher. Both he and

1961–1989 / The Necessary and the Possible

A religious school Bible quiz. Courtesy, NS.

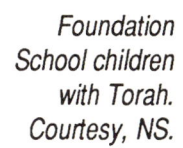

Foundation School children with Torah. Courtesy, NS.

A United Synagogue Youth group, 1963. From left: Bruce Weinsoft, Julie Keller, Gerald Gumbert, and Rich Koplan. Courtesy, NS.

Following A River

Goldie later served as staff there for several summers. Consequently, when the Stampfers arrived in Portland with their three young sons in 1953, they brought with them a joint commitment to the kind of valuable learning experience that the camp environment provides. Together, they decided to translate that commitment into the reality of a camp in the Northwest.

Shortly after arriving in Portland, Rabbi Stampfer met with Rabbi Joseph Wagner of Herzl Synagogue in Seattle and proposed that the two communities jointly sponsor a week-long camp program for high school students. The original camp was held in Seattle at Echo Lake (which, according to Rabbi Stampfer, "sounds lovelier than it was") in a small, rather rundown motel. The program of activities for the 25 or so teenagers who attended included sports such as baseball and swimming; participation in plays, singing, crafts, and Israeli dancing; classes in Hebrew, the Torah, and the history of Israel; and religious services. In addition, the young campers took turns waiting on tables and cleaning the sleeping and public areas.

The following summer, a second week-long session was added for sixth-to-eighth-graders and the camp was formally named after the noted leader of the Conservative movement in the United States, Solomon Schechter. Its name, however, was about the only thing formal about it. Services and meetings were held in a large (borrowed) army surplus tent; the meals were cooked in pots on loan from the synagogue and served on disposable plates at outdoor picnic tables, rain or shine; baseball, for which campers brought their own equipment, was played in a cow pasture, a circumstance which added a whole new meaning to the concept of "flies" in "deep center." These limitations, combined with the facts that the lake was no longer approved for swimming and that the "camp" was on a busy highway, made it clear that Echo Lake was not a desirable location for a permanent camp.

In 1958, the directors and a newly formed camp committee were delighted to learn that Seattle Pacific University had purchased a large, abandoned military base at Fort Casey on Whidbey Island. The barracks, officer's quarters, and other facilities were perfect for the camp's needs, and the committee was quick to make arrangements for renting them. At Fort Casey, the camp program was expanded to five weeks, the youngest campers coming for one week and the intermediate and high school students for two. Over the 11 summers that Camp Solomon Schechter operated on Whidbey

1961–1989 / The Necessary and the Possible

Enjoying a day in the pool at Camp Solomon Schechter, 1961. Below, a typical group of campers, 1973. Courtesy, Rabbi Joshua Stampfer.

Island, a swimming pool was added, all the buildings were painted, and the facilities were generally improved. Gradually, however, simultaneous rentals of the facilities by other groups began to destroy the uniqueness of the environment and once again a search began for a new site.

This time the committee was lucky enough to find one of the finest summer camps in the Pacific Northwest up for sale—Trail's End Camp in Tumwater, Washington. It had 162 acres on a private lake with cabins and a dining hall. To raise money to buy the camp, Rabbi Stampfer worked closely with Dr. Theodore Suher, president of the camp at the time, Ed Moskowitz, president of the United Synagogue region, attorney Maurice Sussman, and other members of Neveh Shalom. In the summer of 1969, the first session at the new campsite was held.

Camp Solomon Schechter, under the successive presidencies of Maurice Sussman, Solomon Menashe, Victor Menashe, Donald Olds and the current directorship of Judy Kahn, has emerged as one of the strongest educational resources in the region, accommodating over 300 campers every summer from the Northwest and around the world. The camp has inspired and given direction to future rabbis, cantors, scholars, and communal leaders in both the U.S. and Israel. As with the Stampfers, the camp experience has also provided the happy occasion for numerous meetings of future husbands and wives. When Rabbi Stampfer retired from active directorship, the lake at Camp Solomon Schechter was named Stampfer Lake in recognition of the tireless, volunteer work that both he and Goldie had put into the camp over the years.

The Grown Children: Continuing Education

As important as the Foundation School, the religious school, and Camp Solomon Schechter have been in the early education of countless Neveh Shalom members, also important have been the educational opportunities available to them as adults. Like the religious school, classes for adults were a tradition long before the 1961 merger, but have flourished and expanded since that time. Since 1980, for example, the adult education classes have been formalized and are now annually described in a substantial catalogue. Besides the traditional classes in the Talmud and the Torah, these classes have come to include a series of book reviews by Rabbi

1961–1989 / The Necessary and the Possible

Stampfer, the proceeds from which have gone to "Stack the Shelves" of the congregational library.

The library itself is one of the main sources of continuing education, not only for members of Neveh Shalom but for the entire Jewish community. When Congregation Neveh Shalom moved to the site on Dosch Road in 1964, a large room was set aside to serve as a library. Leon and Esther Feldstein, longtime members of the congregation, stepped forward and offered to finance the furnishings of this room. Books were transferred from the old building, and the library was named the "Feldstein Library" in honor of their generous gift. Becky Menashe was engaged to serve as the first

Esther Feldstein (left) and librarian Hilde Jacob in Neveh Shalom's Feldstein Library. Esther Feldstein's grandfather, George Gumbert, was among the Neveh Zedek members who stayed with Ahavai Sholom after the short-lived merger in 1895. Courtesy, NS.

librarian, and donations from the congregation rapidly increased the number of volumes. Eventually, a classification system was needed, and Rob Bernstein, then a student at the religious school, developed a unique system as part of his Eagle Scout Award project. Bernstein's system is still in use today.

Under the current librarian, Hilde Jacob, the Feldstein Library holds more than 6,500 titles, plus a considerable music collection on records and tapes and a fledgling assortment of video tapes. All this material is available to congregants and other members of the Portland community, making the Feldstein Library the finest of its kind in Portland, if not the entire Northwest.

As yet another part of its commitment to education, Neveh Shalom has sponsored a continuing series of guest lectureships featuring nationally known religious, intellectual, and political leaders. The list of speakers includes Dr. Mordecai Kaplan, Rabbi Harold Kushner, Dr. Abraham Joshua Heschel, Pinchas Peli, novelist Chaim Potok, and such prominent political figures as Wayne Morse, Abraham Ribicoff, Jacob Javits, and Abba Eban. Complementing this tradition is the "Choose Life" series of monthly speakers initiated during Allan Sherman's presidency in 1985. Over the years these various lecturers have both broadened the horizons of Neveh Shalom members and raised the congregation's stature in the eyes of the community.

One of the most memorable talks given at Neveh Shalom—not so much for its content as for its historical impact—was delivered on May 27, 1968 by a young presidential hopeful from New York, Senator Robert F. Kennedy. Kennedy had arrived in Portland on May 17, 11 days before the Oregon primary in which he and Eugene McCarthy were contenders for the Democratic nomination. Remem-

Sen. Robert F. Kennedy at Neveh Shalom, May 27, 1968. Courtesy, the Oregonian.

bered for his earlier investigation into Portland's vice and labor corruption problems, Kennedy was far from being a popular favorite in the City of Roses. Braving heavy rains and occasional jeers (at one point Kennedy virtually collided with McCarthy at the Portland Zoo and fled in his open convertible to cries of "Coward!"), Kennedy was determined to make up lost ground in Oregon. He was also persuaded by his advisors that he needed to make a major public statement of his support for Israel, and decided to request the pulpit at Neveh Shalom for that purpose.

Despite objections from some quarters about "politicizing" the pulpit, Rabbi Stampfer and President Kurt Hamburger agreed to the Kennedy appearance. And so on May 27, amidst much media coverage and wearing a yarmulka, Kennedy restated his position that "In Israel—unlike so many other places in the world—our commitment is clear and compelling. We are committed to Israel's survival. We are committed to defying any attempt to destroy Israel, whatever the source. And we cannot and must not let that commitment waver."

On the following evening, Kennedy lost the Oregon primary to McCarthy, who won 44.7 percent of the vote. Kennedy's talk at Neveh Shalom was subsequently included in a television report that was seen around the country. According to an Egyptian correspondent named Mahmoud Abel-Hadi, the sight of Kennedy wearing a yarmulka in the synagogue and uttering those words greatly upset one young man in the Pasadena, California home of a Jordanian family. It was reported to the correspondent that the youth "left the room putting his hands on his ears and almost weeping." The young man in question was Sirhan Bishara Sirhan, who, nine days after the Neveh Shalom talk, gunned down Bobby Kennedy as he was taking a shortcut through the pantry area of Los Angeles' Ambassador Hotel. History, like the human heart, has its own version of wisdom.

No discussion of Rabbi Stampfer's educational and religious influence would be complete without mention of the congregation's role in a singularly important trend in modern Jewish life. A report of Neveh Shalom's 1976 social action committee reads in part:

> Starting from the earliest grades we should stress in our religious school that girls are as valuable and important to the Jewish people as boys are. We should reevaluate our texts to be sure that they are not teaching our girls to be second-class citizens instead of fully responsible members of the community.

Following A River

In educating its membership to the changing role of women in Jewish life, the leadership of Congregation Neveh Shalom has been at the forefront of the Conservative movement in the United States. Conservative Judaism, which sees its place as mediating between tradition and change, has, since its 1973 vote permitting women to be counted in the minyan and to be called to the Torah, either encouraged or tolerated a wide range of practice, depending in great part on the individual rabbi. Since arriving in 1953, Rabbi Stampfer has encouraged rather than merely tolerated.

The congregation's first Bat Mitzvah—that of Linda Potter—took place on October 9, 1953, four months after Stampfer's arrival and at his strong urging. Since that time, the list of "firsts" for women has kept pace with the congregation's growth. In 1967, Min Zidell became the first woman to serve on the board; in 1971, Taya Meyer was the first woman officer (secretary); in 1976, Carolyn Weinstein became the first woman to serve as executive director; from 1978 to 1980, Elaine Cogan served as the first woman president of Neveh Shalom (and perhaps the first woman in the United States to precede her husband in such a capacity); and in 1986, Linda Shivers began her tenure as the congregation's first woman cantor. Except for minor resistance from some of the older, more traditional members, all of these firsts for women came about with the support and cooperation of the membership. "When I became the first woman president in 1978," Elaine Cogan recalls, "I have to admit I was somewhat concerned about how I would be accepted, particularly by older members. To my delight, I found them very supportive. The women especially expressed their gladness that the men had finally 'done the right thing.'"

"Finally," here, is a relative term. As early as 1973—early, that is, in the context of the national expansion of rights for Jewish women—the president of the congregation was directed to communicate to the membership "the fact that women and men share equal religious rights in our congregation." The extent of those rights was formalized in the 1976 report of the social action committee mentioned above: young women were to be taught the use of tallit and tefillin and to have the option of using them; mothers were to be called to the Torah for their sons' and daughters' Bar and Bat

Linda Shivers, Neveh Shalom's first and current woman cantor. Courtesy, NS.

Mitzvahs; the wording of the marriage ceremony was to be changed to reflect the equal rights of bride and groom; and women were to be listed in the directory by their own first names. That none of these innovations strikes us as radical today is itself testimony to the effectiveness of the educational process by which they have come to seem routine.

Taken together, then, these various forms of academic and social education have shaped the distinctive tone and character of Congregation Neveh Shalom during the Stampfer era. The literal meaning of *education* is to "bring out," and Rabbi Stampfer's continuing strength has been his ability to bring out the best from the congregation that he has served for the past 35 years.

A Tradition of Doers

"He is not the best leader who is the greatest doer," goes an anonymous saying, "but he who sets others doing with the greatest success." To speak of the "Stampfer era," therefore, is not to suggest that Congregation Neveh Shalom has lacked for successful "doers" since moving to its present site in 1964. The president at that time, Dr. Milton Hasson, stands as the first in a series of officers who have shouldered the burden of leadership with grace, skill, and dedication. A retired dentist who possesses a beautiful singing voice, Hasson has also served as volunteer cantor whenever the congregation has lacked a regular cantor—in one instance, for a period of two years, from 1970 to 1972.

The president during Hasson's two-year term as cantor was Hershal Tanzer, another member who has been an active leader both in the congregation and in the community. It was near the end of Tanzer's first term of office (1970-1972) that the congregation hired full-time cantor and youth director, Marc Dinkin, whose own youth and enthusiasm would be an inspiration to countless members for the next fourteen years. Dinkin was still cantor when Tanzer served his second term as president in 1984-85. Tanzer was also president of the Jewish Federation during the Six-Day War, president of the Jewish National Fund, and president of the Institute for Judaic Studies. A leader in the Oregon timber industry and an avid hiker in Oregon's wilderness, Tanzer also led gubernatorial missions to Israel with

Marc Dinken, cantor of Neveh Shalom from 1972 to 1986. Courtesy, NS.

Following A River

Governors Tom McCall, Bob Straub, Victor Atiyeh, and then-mayor Neil Goldschmidt. His wife, Shirley Tanzer, founded and directed the Oral History Project, an invaluable series of recorded interviews by which the recollections of senior members of the Portland Jewish community are gathered and preserved, and is a leading figure in Holocaust research.

Al Feves, Tanzer's successor, was president (1972-1974) while Rabbi Stampfer was on sabbatical serving as rabbi of the Conservative Center in Jerusalem (Rabbi Stampfer has had three sabbaticals —in 1960, 1967, and 1973—since coming to Ahavai Sholom in 1953, a national record of sorts). When Feves himself traveled to Israel to study the tragic impact of the Yom Kippur War, his first impulse after 13 hours aboard El Al Airline was to call Rabbi Stampfer at his residence in Jerusalem. "Hello, Rabbi, this is your president," Feves announced himself, to which the rabbi replied, "*Who?*" Later Feves realized that in his excitement to contact the rabbi he had called at 3:00 in the morning, which could account for why the rabbi may have momentarily thought that President Nixon, who was then embroiled in Watergate, was calling him for advice. Feves' wife, Sadie, has led many women's organizations in the city, serving with special distinction as president of the Robison Jewish Home Sisterhood.

Among other husband-and-wife teams, Elaine and Arnold Cogan hold the unique distinction of having both served as presidents of the congregation. Elaine Cogan was not only the first, but thus far the only woman president, serving from 1978 to 1980. She has also served as chairwoman of the Portland Development Commission and as president of the Portland League of Women Voters. The author of a book on public speaking, she was also a member of a committee that recently completed a revision of the Friday evening prayerbook.

Arnold Cogan, a highly respected consultant in urban and regional planning, is the current president of Neveh Shalom. He served as State Planning Director under Governor Tom McCall and was the first executive director of the agency that developed Oregon's nationally acclaimed land use laws. In his role as president of the congregation, his approach to problem-solving is Solomon-like—that is, through diplomacy and consensus—though he might also be compared to Noah for having predicted the periodic floods that have plagued the Neveh Shalom parking lot.

Rounding out the Cogan family's contribution to Congregation Neveh Shalom is Arnold's brother, Dr. Gerald Cogan, who served as

1961–1989 / The Necessary and the Possible

president from 1974 to 1976. Like Milton Hasson, Dr. Cogan is a dentist, a coincidence that will inevitably prompt the unfortunate implication that getting someone to serve as president can be like pulling teeth! Dr. Cogan has also played an important role in state politics, serving as the Democratic National Committeeman for the State of Oregon. A man of letters other than the degrees after his name, Dr Cogan has also written several plays.

Elaine, Arnold, and Gerald Cogan. Courtesy, the Cogan family.

Finally, we note two presidents who represent cross-generational service to the congregation: Richard Brownstein (1980-82), who is the grandson of Cantor Hillel Slifman; and Mark Ail (1986-1988), who is the grand-nephew of Cantor Morris Ail. Just as Mark Ail in his youth served as president of the United Synagogue Youth, Dick Brownstein in his youth was national president of the B'nai B'rith Youth Organization (two of his children, Jeb and Jois, were also national presidents). Brownstein has also been district president of B'nai B'rith and president of the Institute for Judaic Studies.

It was during Brownstein's administration that the congregation devised an innovative way of handling the growing administrative tasks that had previously been the responsibility of the executive secretary. As we have seen, Executive Secretary Karl Bettman, who died in 1964, was a hard act to follow. Followed he was, however, by Milton Horenstein, who ably filled that position from 1964 to 1976 (Horenstein continues to serve the congregation as gabbai, along with Philip Shuldman). At this point, the position was expanded to accommodate growing membership, and the title was changed to "executive director" when Carolyn Weinstein took over in 1976. When Brownstein became president in 1980, the position of executive director was held by a young man named Ron Sandler, who proved less impressive to the congregation on the job than he had on paper. Moreover, Sandler's departure on a sour note confirmed the congregation's growing awareness that the responsibilities of the executive director were becoming more than one person could handle.

For a short period in 1981, while the executive board consulted about what to do, Marc Dinken took on the position in addition to his roles as cantor and youth director—just one more of Dinkin's many valuable contributions to the synagogue. Finally, the board came up with what has proved a very successful solution: to divide the 40-hour-a-week job into two 30-hour-a-week jobs to be taken on by two members of the synagogue: Sylvia Pearlman and Sandey Fields. Pearlman became director of membership, in charge of dues, the upkeep of the physical plant and the cemetery, and other business matters; and Fields became programs director, in charge of the *Chronicle*, volunteer services, and the various congregational programs, including continuing education. When Sandey Fields moved away in 1985, the position of programs director was assumed by Sheri Cordova. The current smooth operation of the congregation is a tribute not only to the exceptional talents of Pearlman and Cordova, but to the tradition of innovation that continues to keep Congregation Neveh Shalom young in spirit.

Contributions to any synagogue take other forms than adminstrative service, of course, and one of those is financial support. The major philanthropist of Congregation Neveh Shalom throughout his long career was the late Sam Zidell. Zidell rose from humble origins by dint of hard work and a very incisive mind, eventually attaining great wealth in the scrap metal business. Lavish in his sup-

*Sam Zidell.
Courtesy,
Rose Zidell.*

port of all things Jewish, he often encouraged others to follow suit by offering challenge gifts to various causes. He is remembered by many for his casual manner and rough-house talk. Neveh Shalom's Zidell Chapel, which he endowed, is named in his honor. In more recent time, members such as Jakob Kryzsek and others have carried on the tradition of philanthropy established by Zidell.

The Country of Common Knowledge

Were the list of leaders and contributors to go on, it would have to include those numerous untitled congregants whose work and support keep the river of Congregation Neveh Shalom flowing smoothly. But to attempt this would be to run a risk—not mainly the risk of offending those whom we would inevitably leave out, but rather the risk of turning this history into a guided tour. The proper job of the historian is to explore and discover—in our case, to "follow a river" from its headwaters to where it flows into the country of common knowledge. Having arrived at that country, our job is done.

But in another sense, the job can never be done, because the river keeps moving. Congregation Neveh Shalom will undoubtedly continue to change in many ways, but it will carry with it the detritus of everything that has come before—the squabbles, the hopes, the mistakes, the joys—all of it potential nourishment for generations of Jews to come. True, our "river" is merely a single congregation in one corner of a large country, in a world preoccupied with momentous events and unprecedented challenges. But "Don't be fooled," writes naturalist David Quammen:

> Rivers are important, in the history of life, in the history of man, far beyond their size. Rivers have served as crucibles of evolution, pathways of colonization, sources of power, and inspiration and topsoil. They not only provide, they deliver. Glaciers come and go, lakes fill up and disappear, but rivers continue to follow their chosen routes with exceptional permanence, changing character gradually, maturing, cutting tight canyons and wide valleys, shifting about restlessly within their domains, always wandering, always leaving, never gone; offering to their living inhabitants that one crucial element that survival by evolution demands: time.

Appendices

Rabbis, Cantors, and Presidents

Ahavai Sholom: 1869-1961

Rabbis

Julius Eckman	1869–1872
Marcus Mellis	1880–1882
Rudolph Farber	1897–1898
Wolff Willner	1906–1907
Arthur Montaz	1918–1920
Nahum Krueger	1921–1924
Maurice Teshnor	1924–1925
Elliott Burstein	1926–1927
Herbert Parzen	1928–1932
Raphael Goldenstein	1932–1933
Edward Sandrow	1933–1937
Charles Sydney	1937–1951
Ralph Weissberger	1951–1952
Joshua Stampfer	1952–1961

Cantor/Rabbis

(Served as spiritual leaders in the absence of ordained rabbis.)

S. Arager [?]	1876 [?]
Herman Bories	1879
Robert Abrahamson	1880–1884
I. Kaiser	1884–1885
G. Danziger	1885
Abraham Edelman	1885–1886
Robert Abrahamson	1886–1895
Jacob Blaustein	1895–1898
Robert Abrahamson	1898–1922

Cantors

Hillel Slifman	1923–1925
Morris Ail	1925–1961

Presidents

Newman Goodman	1869–[?]
Leiser Cohn	1873–[?]
William Gallick	[?]–1884
Henry Danziger	1884–1890
Simon Abrahams	1890–1893
Meyer Raphael	1893–1895
David Lewis	1895
Isaac Gevurtz	1895–1896
Isaac Apple	1896–1897
Meyer Raphael	1897
Isaac Gevurtz	1897–1898
Simon Abrahams	1898
Morris Gilbert	1898–1904
Joseph Shemanski	1904–1906
Louis Krause	1906–1908
Abraham Rosenstein	1908–1912
Louis Krause	1912–1918
Alex Miller	1918–1921
Sam Swirsky	1921–1924
Alex Miller	1924–1925
John Dellar	1925–1927
Sam Swirsky	1927–1928
Louis Gevurtz	1928–1931
Nathan Weinstein	1932–1936
Harry Zavin	1936–1940
Louis Gevurtz	1940–1945
James Goldeen	1945–1947
Jack Colton	1947–1951
Erwin Davis	1951–1954
Maurice Sussman	1954–1956
Hy Solko	1956–1957
Philip Weinstein	1957–1959
Hy Solko	1959–1960
Louis Rosenberg	1960–1961

Appendix

Neveh Zedek: 1892–1901

Cantors

Jacob Blaustein	1892–1895, 1898
I. Goldstein	1899
Mendel Cohen	1901

Presidents

L. Jacobs	1894–1895

(Merged with Ahavai Sholom, 1895–1896.)

Talmud Torah: 1893–1901

Rabbis

N. Mosessohn	1899–1901

Cantors

Max Levin	1896–1901

Presidents

M. Rosenstein	1893–1894
H. Gertzman	1895
M. Simon	1897–1898
William Fest	1899
Maurice Ostrow	1900–1901

Neveh Zedek Talmud Torah*: 1902–1961

Rabbis

N. Mosessohn	1902
Adolph Abbey	1904–1905
Henry Heller	1907–1911
Samuel Sachs	1922–1927
Meyer Rubin	1928–1933
Abraham Israelitan	1934
Albert Ruskin	1935–1936
Philip Kleinman	1937–1955
Norman Siegel	1956–1957
Jack Segal	1958–1961

Cantors

Mendel Cohen	1902
I. Medvedovsky	1903
J. Shapo	1905–1906
A. Rosencrantz	1915–1936
Joseph Freeman	1938–1961

*Referred to as "Neveh Zedek."

Presidents

Maurice Ostrow	1902–1904
Isaac Apple	1904
David Nemerovsky	1905–1909
Marcus Gale	1910–1912
David Nemerovsky	1913–1914
Louis Shank	1915–1916
David Nemerovsky	1917–1924
Marcus Gale	1925–1928
George Rubenstein	1929
Jacob Asher	1930–1931
Louis Shank	1932
Marcus Gale	1933–1934
Morris Goldblatt	1935–1938
Sidney Stern	1939–1940
Abraham Gilbert	1941–1947
Lawrence Gale	1948–1950
Ben Steinberg	1951–1953
Harry Jackson	1954–1958
Si Cohn	1959–1961

Appendix

Neveh Shalom: 1961–present

Rabbis

Joshua Stampfer	1961–present

Cantors

Arthur Yolkoff	1961–1962
Chaim Feifel	1962–1967
Albert Mulgay	1967–1968
Joseph Tauman	1968–1969
Milton Hasson	1970–1972
Marc Dinken	1972–1986
Linda Shivers	1986–present

Presidents

Louis Rosenberg	1961–1962
Lou Olds	1962–1964
Milton Hasson	1964–1966
Kurt Hamburger	1966–1968
Ted Suher	1968–1970
Hershal Tanzer	1970–1972
Al Feves	1972–1974
Gerald Cogan	1975–1976
Norman Wapnick	1976–1978
Elaine Cogan	1978–1980
Richard Brownstein	1980–1982
Allan Sherman	1982–1984
Hershal Tanzer	1984–1985
Allan Sherman	1985–1986
Mark Ail	1986–1988
Arnold Cogan	1988–present

Sisterhood Presidents

Elizabeth Weinstein	1927–1930
Sarah Hodes	1933–1935
Rose Swire	1935–1937
Mary Haimo	1938–1940
Belle Gevurtz	1940–1944
Mary Abrams	1944
Tillie Jacobson	1945–1946
Rose Zidell	1947–1948
Sarah Davis	1949–1950
Ann Gerstenfeld	1950–1953
Florence Colton	1953–1954
Nina Weinstein	1954–1955
Raye Friedman	1955–1957
Mary Rosenberg	1957–1958
Min Zidell	1958–1960
Tillie Caplan	1960–1961
Min Zidell	1961–1962
Florence Cohen	1962–1963
Fritzie Sussman	1963–1965
Gladys Fendel	1965–1968
Ruth Hopfer	1968–1969
Gladys Fendel	1969–1970
Marie Leton	1970–1972
Beverly Eastern	1972–1975
Darlene Shemarya	1975–1976
Gladys Fendel	1976
Lucille Frost	1976–1978
Ellen Darr	1978–1981
Carol Rogat	1981–1983
Carole Rotstein	1983–1985
Laurie Weinsoft	1985–1987
Esther Menashe	1987–1989

Appendix

(Neveh Shalom, continued)

Men's Club Presidents

E. R. Nudelman	1939 (Founder)
D. Fertig	1939–1940
Erwin Davis	1940
David Friedman	[?]
Louis Heckman	[?]
Max Freeman	1948–1949
Irvin Kane	1949–1950
Edward Kameny	1951–1953
Edward Potter	1953–1954
Nathan Weinstein	1954–1956
Barrie Itkin	1956–1958
Nathan Ail	1958–1961
Milton Hasson	1961–1962
Jerome Semler	1962–1964
Edward Moskowitz	1964–1965
Norman Wapnick	1965–1966
Ivor Levy	1966–1968
Ed Srebnik	1968–1969
Jack Lakefish	1969–1970
Richard Jolosky	1970–1971
Ivor Levy	1971–1972
Allan Sherman	1972–1974
Samuel Sadis	1974–1976
Arnold Westerman	1976–1977
Mark Ail	1977–1980
Gary Weinstein	1980–1982
Peter Pressman	1983
Ron Morris	1983–1986
Steve Cooper	1986–1988
Ron Morris	1988–present

USY Chapter Presidents

Tommy Mandler	1953
Arden Shenker	1954
Allan Campf	1955
Joe Rubin	1956
Ron Weinstein	1956
Keith Koplan	1958
Larry Volchok	1959
Howard Liebreich	1960
J. Verbin, M. Goldberg	1961
R. Koplan, G. Gumbert	1962
Alice Witokowski	1963
Mary Ellen Rubin	1963
Michael Goldberg	1964
Mark Ail	1966
Dave Lippoff	1967
JoAnne Blauer	1968
Elton Mandler	1969
Jack Birnbach	1970
JoAnne Menashe	1971
Debbie Lohman	1972
Bill Schauffer	1973
Geri Moskowitz	1974
D. Samuels, K. Young	1975
Jeff Weinstein	1976
Perri Floom	1977
Tom Meyer	1978
Dave Rubin	1979
Don Jacob	1980
Larry Holzman	1981
Dan Cogan	1982
Richard Meyer	1983
Sarah Kahn	1984
Sam Zalutsky	1985
Ronette Levy	1986
Jody Linn	1987
Ali Jaffe	1988

Sources

Newspapers

American Hebrew News
American Israelite
Hebrew Observer
Jewish Tribune
Oregon Journal
Oregonian
Scribe

Research Sites

Jewish Historical Society of Oregon
Multnomah County Public Library
Neveh Shalom Archives
The Oregon Historical Society
Reed College Library

Selected Bibliography

Blumenthal, Helen E. "The New Odessa Colony of Oregon, 1882-1886." *Western States Jewish Historical Quarterly*, July, 1982.

Cline, Scott. "The Jews of Portland, Oregon. A Statistical Dimension, 1860-1880." *Oregon Historical Quarterly*, Vol. 88, No. 1, 5-25.

Cline, Scott. "Creation of An Ethnic Community: Portland Jewry 1857-1866." *Pacific Northwest Quarterly*, Vol. 76, No. 2, 52-60.

Dawidowicz, Lucy S. *The War Against the Jews: 1933-1945*. New York: Holt, Rinehart and Winston, 1975.

Dimont, Max I. *Jews, God and History*. New York: New American Library, 1962.

Friedlander, Israel. *The Jews of Russia and Poland*. New York: G. P. Putnam's Sons, 1915.

Sources

Glanz, Rudolf. "Vanguard to the Russians: The Poseners in America." *Yivo Annual of Jewish Social Science*, Vol. 18, 1-38.

Goldberg, Deborah B. *Jewish Spirit on the Urban Frontier: Zionism in Portland, Oregon 1901-1941.* B.A. thesis, Reed College, 1982.

Gould, Stephen Jay. "Science and Jewish Immigration." *Hen's Teeth and Horse's Toes*, Chap. 22. New York: W. W. Norton, 1983.

Kramer, William M. "David Solis-Cohen of Portland: Patriot, Pietist, Litterateur and Lawyer." *Western States Jewish Historical Quarterly*, Vol. 14, No. 2, 139-166.

Lowenstein, Steven. *The Jews of Oregon 1850-1950.* Portland: Jewish Historical Society of Oregon, 1987.

MacColl, E. Kimbark, Jr. *The Shaping of a City: Business and Politics in Portland, Oregon 1885-1915.* Portland: The Georgian Press, 1976.

Nodel, Rabbi Julius J. *The Ties Between: A Century of Judaism on America's Last Frontier.* Portland, 1959.

Schneider, Susan Weidman. *Jewish and Female.* New York: Simon and Schuster, 1984.

Stampfer, Rabbi Joshua. *Pioneer Rabbi of the West: The Life and Times of Julius Eckman.* Portland, 1988.

Steinberg, Milton. *Basic Judaism.* New York: Harcourt Brace Jovanovich, 1947.

Stern, Norton B. and William M. Kramer. "Jewish Padre to the Pueblo: Pioneer Los Angeles Rabbi Abraham Wolf Edelman." *Western States Jewish Historical Quarterly*, Vol. 3, No. 4, 206-220.

Toll, William. *The Making of an Ethnic Middle Class: Portland Jewry Over Four Generations.* Albany: State University of New York Press, 1982.

Vanden Heuvel, William, and Milton Gwirtzman. *On His Own: Robert F. Kennedy, 1964-1968.* Doubleday & Co., Inc.: Garden City, New York, 1970.

Witcover, Jules. *85 Days: The Last Campaign of Robert Kennedy.* G. P. Putnam's Sons: New York, 1969.

Index of Persons

[This index does not include persons whose names appear only in the preface, the appendix, or as illustration acknowledgments.]

Abel-Hadi, Mahmoud, 141
Abbey, Rabbi Adolph, 42
Abrahams, Simon, 49, 50
Abrahamson, Anna, 66
Abrahamson, Rev. Robert, 27-28, 30, 31, 32, 37-38, 42, 48, 62, 65-68
Abrams, S. H., 50
Ail, Mark, 134, 145
Ail, Morris, 83-84, 86, 145
Alexander II, 36
Alexander III, 36
Allen, Woody, 120
Apple, Isaac, 43
Arager, S., 26
Asher, Adolph, 105
Asher, Jacob, 79-80
Atiyeh, Victor, 144
Balfour, Arthur James, 74
Barocas, Nat, 126
Batt, Jacob, 16, 18
Ben-Gurion, David, 108
Berkham, Nathan, 82-83
Berkowitz, Rabbi Henry, 98
Bernstein, Rob, 139
Bernstein, Salome, 61
Bettman, Kaete, 100
Bettman, Karl, 100-103, 114, 126, 145
Bettman, Max, 100
Bettman, Samuel, 100, 101
Bishoff, Sol, 57
Blaustein, Rev. Jacob, 37-42
Blumenthal, Cele, 122
Bonaparte, Napoleon, 10
Bories, Herman, 26
Boskowitz, Anselm, 57, 95, 96, 99, 100
Brownstein, Richard, 145, 146
Burstein, Rabbi Elliott, 78
Campf, Fritzie Sussman, 124, 129
Caplan, Sam, 83-84
Catherine the Great, 36
Chusid, Beatrice Scheuer, 94, 99
Cline, Scott, 16
Cogan, Arnold, 124, 144
Cogan, Elaine, 142, 144
Cogan, Dr. Gerald, 144-145
Cohen, Frieda Gass, 53

Cohen, Mrs. Isaac Lesser, 61
Cohn, Julius, 62
Cohn, Leiser, 16-18
Cohn, Si, 120, 121, 122
Cordova, Sheri, 146
Crook, George, 23
Danziger, Rev. G. A., 30, 31
Danziger, Henry, 30, 43
Danziger, Moses, 34
Davis, Dan, 123
Davis, Erwin "Ike," 110, 114
Dellar, John, 56, 75
Dellar, Solomon, 75
De Mille, Cecil B., 129
Dinken, Marc, 143, 146
Eban, Abba, 140
Eckman, Rabbi Julius, 13, 20-25, 30, 33, 85, 91, 134
Edelman, Rev. Abraham W., 31-32
Failing, Henry, 23
Fain, Rabbi Joseph, 72, 98
Feifel, Chaim, 125
Feldstein, Esther, 139
Feldstein, Leon, 126, 139
Fendel, Betty Lynn, 131
Feves, Al, 144
Feves, Sadie, 144
Fields, Sandey, 146
Franklin, Marx, 16
Freeman, Joseph, 103
Friedman, Max, 66-67
Gale, Lawrence, 81
Gale, Marcus, 53, 80-81, 90
Gaynor, Rabbi Nathan, 111
Gevurtz, Alec, 46
Gevurtz, Cacelie Gerson, 46
Gevurtz, Harry, 47, 99
Gevurtz, Isaac, 43, 45-48, 81, 86
Gevurtz, Lillian, 46
Gevurtz, Louis, 46, 47, 81, 85-87, 91, 120
Gevurtz, Mae, 46
Gevurtz, Matthew, 46
Gevurtz, Milton, 46
Gibbs, J., 23
Gilbert, Morris, 48, 51, 56
Glanz, Rudolph, 13

Goddard, H. H., 69
Goldberg, Deborah, 74
Goldschmidt, Neil, 144
Goldsmith, Jacob, 9
Goodman, Newman, 16, 18, 25, 43
Goodman, Jules Eckman, 25
Goldenstein, Rabbi Raphael, 83
Goldstein, Charles, 16, 18
Greenberg, Joseph Maxwell, 132
Greenberg, Kate Swire, 132
Gumbert, George, 139
Gumbert, Gerald, 135
Gumbert, Grayce, 133
Hamburger, Kurt, 128, 141
Harris, Anna, 25
Harris, Joseph, 16, 18, 25, 37
Hasson, Dr. Milton, 143, 145
Heller, Rabbi Henry Jacob, 42, 74, 75, 82
Herzl, Theodor, 76
Heschel, Dr. Abraham, 140
Hirsch, Max, 99
Hitler, Adolph, 90, 99
Hodes, Blossom, 132
Hodes, Francine, 132
Hodes, Michael, 132
Hodes, Sarah Swire, 132
Hodes, Stan, 132
Holzman, the brothers, 65
Horenstein, Eleanor, 133
Horenstein, Milton, 145-146
Israelitan, Rabbi Abraham, 82
Itkin, Suzanne Gevurtz, 85
Jackson, Harry, 121
Jacob, Alma, 98
Jacob, Heinz, 97-98
Jacob, Hilde, 139
Jacob, Siegfried, 98
Javits, Jacob, 140
Kahn, Judy, 138
Kaiser, I., 28-30
Kaplan, Dr. Mordecai, 140
Keller, Irma, 134
Keller, Julie, 135
Kennedy, Robert F., 140-141
Kleinman, Mathew, 64
Kleinman, Rabbi Philip, 64-65, 76, 82, 98, 103-105, 117
Kohs, Sam, 57
Koplan, Rich, 135
Krueger, Rabbi Nahum, 65, 70, 71-72
Kryzsek, Jakob, 147
Kushner, Rabbi Harold, 140
Ladd, W. S., 23
Lauterstein, Jacob, 57, 75

Lauterstein, Paula Heller, 74-75
Lazarus, E., 50
Lee, Dorothy McCullogh, 110
Lesman, Max, 110
Lesman, Rose Swire, 132
Lesman, Sol, 132
Levin, Phillip, 16, 18
Lipman, Sigmund, 57
Margulis, Milton, 57
May, Lewis, 9
McCall, Tom, 144
McCarthy, Eugene, 140-141
McKinley, William, 48
Meier, Julius, 80
Meir, Golda, 76, 91
Mellis, Frederick, 26
Mellis, Rev. Marcus, 26-28, 31
Mellis, Theo, 26
Menashe, Albert, 131
Menashe, Becky, 139
Menashe, Solomon, 138
Menashe, Victor, 138
Menashe, Toinette, 75, 87, 91, 133
Mendelsohn, Sam, 57
Mendelssohn, Moses, 12
Merrin, Jackie, 134
Meyer, Taya, 142
Miller, Alex, 56, 99
Minevitch, Shirley Hodes, 132
Mittleman, Harry, 99
Moffatt, Richard, 129
Montaz, Rabbi Arthur, 63-63
Morse, Wayne, 140
Mosessohn, Nehemiah, 41
Moskowitz, Ed, 138
Nemerovsky, David, 53, 80-81
Neuberger, Richard, 115
Nixon, Richard, 120, 144
Nodel, Rabbi Julius, 59
Nudelman, Joseph, 75
Nudelman, Hy, 107, 11
Olds, Donald, 138
Olds, Lou, 124, 128
Ostrow, Maurice, 52, 81
Palley, Ben, 65
Parzen, Rabbi Herbert, 76, 78-79, 82-83
Pearlman, Sylvia, 146
Peli, Pinchas, 140
Potok, Chaim, 140
Potter, Irv, 106
Potter, Linda, 142
Prag, Raphael, 16, 18, 19
Pruitt, Major, 126-127
Pruitt, Viola, 126, 127

Raphael, Meyer, 39-40, 43
Reinhardt, Gussie, 108
Ribicoff, Abraham, 140
Rich, Jess, 57
Robinson, David, 90
Rosenberg, Abraham "English," 121, 122, 124
Rosenberg, Louis, 121, 122
Rosencrantz, Abraham, 53-56, 82, 126, 128
Rosenstein, Abe, 62
Rothschild, Lord Walter, 74
Rubenstein, Esy, 45
Rubenstein, Dr. George, 79
Rubin, Ben, 57
Rubin, Leah, 134
Rubin, Rabbi Meyer, 80
Ruskin, Rabbi Albert, 81, 82
Sachs, Rabbi Samuel, 72, 80-82
Sandler, Ron, 146
Sandrow, Rabbi Edward, 88-90
Schwab, Rabbi Isaac, 13
Schechter, Solomon, 62, 136
Scheuer, Celia 94
Scheuer, Ernest, 93-96
Scheuer, Hedwig, 93-96, 99
Scheuer, Sally, 93-96, 99
Schlosberg, William, 70
Schwarz, Maurice, 102
Semler, Leon, 65
Shattuck, Judge, 30
Shecter, J. J., 85
Shemanski, Joseph, 56, 57
Sherman, Allan, 140
Shivers, Linda, 142
Shuldman, Philip, 106-107, 146
Sichel, Sig, 49
Segal, Rabbi Jack, 117, 120, 121
Segal, Toby, 121
Siegel, Rabbi Norman, 117
Singer, Abie, 70
Sirhan, Sirhan Bishara, 141
Slifman, Hillel, 84, 145
Solis-Cohen, David, 50, 57-61, 72, 79
Solko, Hy, 114, 121
Spigal, David, 45
Stampfer, Elana, 113
Stampfer, Goldie, 113-114, 134-136, 138
Stampfer, Rabbi Joshua, 112-117, 122, 123, 125, 127, 130, 133-138, 141, 143
Stampfer, Meir, 113
Stampfer, Nehama, 113
Stampfer, Noam, 113

Stampfer, Shaul, 113
Steinberg, Harriet, 133
Stern, Jerry, 124
Stern, Sidney, 105
Stone, Simon, 25
Straub, Bob, 144
Suher, Ethel, 134
Suher, Dr. Theodore, 138
Sussman, Maurice, 114, 121, 138
Swett, Isaac, 43-45, 51-52, 56, 60, 61
Swett, Julia, 44-45
Swett, Meyer, 45
Swett, Zeke, 57
Swire, George, 132
Swire, Mel, 132
Swire, Preva Sax, 132
Swirsky, Fruma, 132
Swirsky, Max, 132
Swirsky, Sam, 70, 77, 78, 85, 132
Sydney, Rabbi Charles, 98, 100-102, 111
Tanzer, Hershal, 143-144
Tanzer, Shirley, 106, 144
Teshnor, Maurice, 77
Thoreau, Henry David, 7-9
Tice, J. M., 19
Toll, William, 71, 77, 85, 108
Tonkin, Sam, 57
Trachtenburg, Gladys Goodman, 18
Trachtenburg, John, 18
Wagner, Rabbi Joseph, 136
Wapnick, Norman, 124, 128
Wax, Saul, 114
Weinbaum, Edward, 57
Weiner, Dave, 121, 122, 124
Weinsoft, Bruce, 135
Weinsoft, Marcia Swire, 132
Weinstein, Alex, 57
Weinstein, Carolyn, 142, 146
Weinstein, Dave, 124
Weinstein, Moe, 65
Weinstein, Nathan, 57, 62, 63, 99
Weinstein, Mrs. Nathan, 85
Weinstein, Philip, 110, 121
Weinstein, Samuel, 90
Weissberger, Rabbi Ralph, 110, 111
"White Cloud, Chief," 66-67
Wildman, A., 77
Willmer, Rabbi Wolff, 62
Wise, Rabbi Jonah, 57, 60, 62, 72, 83
Wise, Rabbi Stephen, 47, 48, 76, 83
Yolkoff, Arthur, 84
Zidell, Min, 142
Zidell, Sam, 114, 146

Publication of this history of Congregation Neveh Shalom was made possible by a generous grant from Stella Klebe.

On moving to Portland and joining Congregation Neveh Shalom in 1973, Stella Klebe made the synagogue the focus of her life, attending services daily and participating in every offering of the Adult Education Program. For many years, she organized a monthly Rosh Hodesh celebration at morning services, attending personally to every detail.

During her long life, Ms. Klebe has faced many hardships, including escape from Nazi Europe under perilous circumstances. Completely devoted to Israel, she campaigned vigorously at the United Nations when the critical vote on the partition of Palestine took place.

In honor of the forthcoming celebration of her 90th birthday—on December 28, 1989—Ms. Klebe assured the publication of this book by her gift. Her blessings, in addition to longevity, include a devoted daughter, Ellen Kaim, and two granddaughters.